A Garland of Daisies

a Jersey Childhood

A Garland of Daisies

a Jersey childhood

by

Margaret Vaudin

Regency Press (London & New York) Ltd.
125 High Holborn, London WC1V 6QA

ISBN 0 7212 0669 7

Printed and bound in Great Britain by
Buckland Press Ltd., Dover, Kent.

Contents

For
'Mary, With Love'
(looking back over six decades)

CHAPTER ONE

Georgian Childhood 1921-1934

I know I am a "Georgian" because one of my earliest memories is of seeing King George V. I was four years old and it was in 1921, which was a real summer, that might have rivalled our own real summer of 1976.

I was wearing a cream shantung coat and a leghorn straw hat with a garland of daisies round the crown. I loved this outfit immoderately but pride of possession went to my little silk Union Jack. I knew I had to wave this for the King, who, with Queen Mary and Princess Mary were visiting Jersey, where I was born.

Imagine, then, my bewilderment, when a series of horsedrawn carriages began to pass, filled with ladies and gentlemen, none of whom were wearing anything remotely resembling a crown. In horror, in case I missed the magical moment when I must wave to my King, I shrieked as loudly as I could; "But which is the King?"

Consternation from my parents but glee from me when a dark-haired, bearded gentleman, heard, glanced up smilingly and saluted *me!* I have been an ardent royalist ever since.

My second clear recollection of my young life was far from happy. I blush even now to think of it. I had been exceptionally naughty. Years and years later, I asked my mother why she had not beaten me. She replied, "My way was much better. You never forgot, did you?" Too true I never forgot it. Sixty years later it is as clear as it was all those years ago.

I was nearly five, and we were moving house. My mother had gone to the new house to check on something the workman were doing, and had taken me with her.

"Now, Margaret," my mother instructed me, "On no account must you touch the staircase paint. It is still wet." And off she went

My mother's home, "Cedars" Kidderminster.

The house where my sister and I were born in Jersey.

downstairs to the basement kitchen. It was a most inconvenient house with unexpected stairs and odd corners and four floors lit by gas.

As soon as she had disappeared, I had a good look at the paint. It was so lovely and shiny, I *had* to touch it, and the result was two little brown fingers. I can remember feeling a little bit scared, and, idiot child that I was, saw fit to wipe my fingers clean on the newly wall-papered wall in the hall. Worse was to follow, because I then said it was not me! Mothers have sometimes told me since, that children do not learn to lie until they go to school. I must have been very precocious. I lied with a will that day, and I certainly had not started school.

The decorator said, "Don't worry, Mrs. Vaudin. I can make the damage good in a matter of minutes. I have another roll of paper."

To his amazement my mother replied, "Please leave it alone. I want it to stay just as it is. Perhaps Margaret will remember not to be disobedient in future." Those finger marks were there for years!

Another time I can remember my mother was really cross with me. We had a penny-a-week pocket money when we were very small, and I had saved up for two weeks to buy my sister a twopenny bar of chocolate for her birthday. My mother always bought a proper present for us to give each other, but we were expected to make some individual effort. Most unfortunately, we had a bit of a barney the day before her birthday. I was so mad with her, I hid in the spare room where the presents were, and ate the whole bar of chocolate. A twopenny bar was quite big in those far off happy days. It is a pity I cannot report that I was very sick. I was not, as it happens, but I can still see my mother's hurt expression that a child of hers could sink so low!

I sometimes wonder if my poor parents thought they had hatched something not quite normal when they contemplated their second child when young. Before I went to school I was always acting out somebody. With my father I was Mr. Jenkins. With my mother I was Mrs. May. When alone I was two people, who rejoiced in the names of Mavis and Gladys. I cannot for the life of me imagine why I had to be all these people, but they were very real to me and my parents were incredibly patient playing out these characters with me.

My father was dark-haired and brown-eyed. He was clean-shaven and slim. He was as tall as mother but appeared slightly shorter because she wore her hair in a bun on top of her head. Mother put on weight very easily (as I do), but father's weight never varied by so much as an ounce. My mother was fair-haired and blue-eyed and she was very pretty. She

My parents and sister 1918. Me in my father's arms; Jersey.

had quite a commanding presence and did not suffer fools gladly. Father was more tolerant and his dry sense of humour was much appreciated by my mother. They made a very good-looking pair.

One of the earliest indirect influences on our early years was Joseph. In 1910, speaking no word of any language but English, my mother set off for Russia to teach English to a little Polish boy, the son of Countess Mankowska. When other children had such classics as *Little Red Riding Hood* read to them by their bored parents, we used to clamour for stories about Joseph. Pictures showed him to be a fair-headed child, usually dressed in a sailor suit. Imagine how thrilled my mother was in 1947 when Joseph appeared in our new home in Kidderminster with his English wife.

"The only way I could persuade him to come with me to England," she told my mother, "Was by promising to find you." When we complimented him on his near-perfect English, he bowed to my mother and kissed her hand. He was the most charming man and exceptionally good-looking.

He had survived a revolution and two world wars and he had not a shred of anything belonging to his old home. My mother had piles of letters and photographs which she had always treasured, and Joseph was overjoyed. He was then travelling as a displaced person without a passport, but he was about to take out French nationality because he was then living in Dakar, French West Africa.

His mother, Madame Mankowska, (she had dropped her title before the first world war), was a good landlord and cared for her people, starting schools and clinics on her estates, far ahead of her time. There was a very large household including a Polish governess (Miss Dobrewolska), and a Polish tutor for the two elder children, Mary and Karol. When the family travelled about the continent, which they did extensively, my mother made it sound like a royal progress. She greatly enjoyed the two years she spent with the Mankowskas and in 1912, came home for a holiday meaning to return to Russia to teach two little girls, the daughters of Princess Warenska. However, she became engaged to my father instead. It was as well for her that she did not go back as 1914 was beginning to loom over the horizon. My mother was thirty-two when she was married and my father was three years younger.

She brought back some of those delightful wooden dolls that unscrew in the middle and have smaller and ever smaller dolls inside. We called them "Susies" and I played with these dolls endlessly when recovering from my never-ending "bad turns". I still have these dolls and even after seventy years they still maintain their lovely clear painted colours.

I went to kindergarten when I was five. One of the children there had a very bad stammer. My mother maintained I did not have a trace of a stammer until I went to school. I do not know if I subconsciously copied this little boy or whether I did it with an odd feeling of sympathy, but I certainly began to stammer and to this day I have difficulty with my Rs.

It was a dear little school. Miss Labalestier was an old friend of my parents and the school was held in her own house. She was a Froebel Teacher. If possible she liked to keep the numbers even to six little girls and six little boys.

My sister, Roselle, went to a different school. She was a most beautiful baby and grew up to be an exceptionally pretty girl. She was a blonde with hazel eyes and patrician nose. Mine turned up! She had a lovely complexion and dark eyebrows which was odd in a blonde but they gave her a most distinctive look.

Roselle was three-and-a-half years older than me and she had homework at her school, so I demanded homework too. The teacher must have thought me a perfect pest. I remember she wore a black velvet ribbon tied round her head with her hair neatly tucked into this ribbon. One day I was misbehaving in singing class. Miss Labalestier was seated with her back to us, playing the piano, when she suddenly paralysed me by saying, "Margaret, behave. I can see you. You didn't know I had eyes in the back of my head, did you?" I was terrified as I thought she must have another pair of eyes concealed in her ribbon hair-style.

Once we had a Christmas play and I was a fairy. My mother was in the audience and was appalled to see me gradually growing a very unbecoming green colour, as I was wont to do whenever I was excited, prior to a hearty bout of sickness. She had me called off the stage because her nerves could not bear the suspense.

I was led up stairs to the loo, protesting every step of the way. "There was no *need* to make me come off the stage. I could have *lasted*." It was a long time before I forgave her.

My sick turns were an everlasting torment to me. I missed so many treats, parties and picnics. At eight years old, at my next school, I had the first traumatic experience, which left its mark for the rest of my life.

Normally, I think I was a biddable child but on this particular morning I was diabolical. It was in the drawing and painting class and I did not do a stroke of work myself, nor did I allow my friend, Marjorie, to do any either. I spilt her paint water, and hid her india rubber, broke her pencil points and poked her with my ruler, convulsed with idiotic giggling the whole time. I cannot think what the teacher was doing to let me get away with it. However, I was brought down to earth with a bump during the next lesson. It was arithmetic, and suddenly, I could not see the figures in my book, nor could I make out what was written on the blackboard. I was honestly convinced that God had struck me blind for being so naughty to poor Marjorie.

The next thing was "break" and I was in such a state by this time I burst into tears. "I can't see," I sobbed, "I can't see!"

A "big girl" took me home and my sight did not clear until I started being sick, which went on for untold hours. I have suffered this all my life and it was not until I was nearly forty that I was diagnosed as a sufferer from migraine. My poor family had to put up with what was charitably known as "Marg's bad turns", usually at the most inconvenient times.

Another very early memory comes to mind when I was having one of my "bad turns". I had been sick for days. Our own doctor was away so a dear old gentleman called Dr. Rate came to see me.

My dolls (not the wooden Susies) were sitting up in a line at the foot of the bed facing me. The doctor took their temperatures and felt their pulses and, as far as I can recall, took no notice of me at all. I thought he was a lovely doctor to be so kind to my dolls, until he turned to my mother and said, "I don't think there is much wrong with her. Feed her on a light diet for a day or two."

I could not believe my ears. I shot up in bed and said in a furious voice, "I'm four. I can feed myself!" I went off that doctor very quickly, especially when he and my mother laughed.

Another incident in my early childhood which took a lot of living down happened one Christmas Eve. As a pre-Christmas treat my parents were in the habit of going to an hotel for lunch on Christmas Eve, and as soon as Roselle and I were old enough to appreciate (and behave) we went along, too. My father was frequently heard to mutter, "Must we go? I prefer my own restaurant." Meaning no place like home but we all went along happily enough.

I should think it was probably the first time I had been admitted to

My mother in Russia with her Polish Pupil Joseph, 1910.

My father and I in Norway, 1929.

this treat, and for some reason known only to myself, I took exception to the soup.

My mother said gently, "I think you ought to try and drink your soup. It might hurt the chef's feelings if you leave it. Or he might even be cross."

"But I don't like it," I whined. At that precise moment a chef (the chef?) suddenly appeared in our midst. Never did a child fall upon its food with such reckless speed. The sight of the tall white hat and fierce black beard scared me out of my wits!

I had a very happy childhood. I think our upbringing was sensible and well-balanced. The cinema was at its zenith and most children went to the pictures on Saturday afternoons. My mother thought that good fresh sea air was much more important, so summer and winter alike, we went on to the beach. The only exceptions made for going to the cinema were to see Charlie Chaplin and Jackie Coogan. My sister and I developed into rosy-cheeked youngsters and later strapping young women. We hardly had any childish infectious ailments, but in later years when I caught German measles at the age of twenty-three, and measles proper when I was over thirty, I wished mother had not taken such care to keep us in the good sea air!

I recall being a little mortified, but not very much, when I was the only child in my form who had not seen *Peter Pan* at the cinema, but we had such fun on the beach we never knew what we were missing.

We did, however, catch whooping cough, which Roselle picked up after she went to school. I remember one or other of my parents sleeping on a put-you-up bed between us, and sitting up holding a basin in each hand when we were both sick at night. My father took charge of us one day and sent mother out for a breath of air. The doctor came whilst she was out and I can remember sitting on his knee in my little pink dressing-gown. He should have known better, when dealing with me! I threw up all over him. I believe my father felt like killing me! Roselle was much more ill than I and took a long time to recover her normal robust health.

We used to go for a week at Easter and at Whitsuntide to a little cottage perched high up on a cliff with a lovely view over the sea to France, only fourteen miles away at that point. This little holiday home had no mod cons, we had lamps and candles to go to bed, and the landlady cooked on a paraffin stove and a coal range. The loo was a long way down a steep path which we thought was very exciting. I suppose

My sister, 1914.

My sister, 1916.

distance lends enchantment because I really never remember any offensive smell. Most certainly no chemicals were used, unless perhaps a little lime.

We had a wonderful time shrimping in the rock pools and taking them back to be cooked for our tea. Mrs. Le Cocq, the landlady, charged mother two pounds a week for rent and service, and mother bought all the food. What bliss!

The beach at the bottom of the hill was stony but with fascinating rocks to climb. We would spend hours playing shop, collecting yellow shells for butter and white stones for eggs and so on. The pools were full of gorgeous sea anemones and many different types of seaweed. This beach was called Fliquet, and there was another one just around the headland called La Coupe. Neither place ever had any one else but us around. If it was low tide we scrambled across the rocks to La Coupe, but if the tide was in, we had to take a path along the cliff. I have no recollection of any of us being buried under mountains of picnic gear or bathing things. This is strange as we used to go for the day. For a treat, sometimes we would collect driftwood and fry "bacon over the coals" which was mother's name for the operation. The bacon used to be covered in smoke and ash, having frequently dropped off the stick into the fire, and I can say now that I have never tasted anything half as good!

There was a great breakwater nearby, which had been the beginning of a huge harbour, built, I have a feeling, at the time of the Napoleonic Wars. When the one side had been completed, it was discovered that there was not enough water for a harbour after all. (The ground-nut scheme was not the first government blunder!) A lighthouse had been built on the end of the arm that had been finished, and imagine our glee when the lighthouseman sometimes invited us to help him light the lamp. It was all done by hand, of course, and two happier children would have been hard to find!

There was a special place at Rozel (the place after which my sister was named), which served lobster lunches. I seem to remember a rock pool where we could choose our own lobster. Once each holiday we walked over the cliffs and partook of this extra-special treat. We had no car then and it must have been three or four miles there and the same to come back.

My father's family was a very old Jersey family dating back to 1260. In the volume called the *Jersey Armorial* there are six generations of

My sister and I, June 1919.

Vaudins rejoicing in the christian name of Noah. Between the years of 1600 and 1781 it was an unbroken tradition. It was a brave man who stepped out of line and called his eldest son John. My father was an only son and so was my grandfather, so the name dies out with this generation.

My paternal grandfather was a terrifying old gentleman He objected strongly to any form of change or progress. Thus, no mod cons, were allowed in his house. This consisted of thirty-two rooms and is now a boys' school. My three unmarried aunts had to wrestle with lamps and candles. They cooked on a coal range or open wood fire. There was no running water except for a cold tap in the scullery. There was an indoor loo, though, which boasted a glorious mahogany seat with a pull-up lever to flush. The pan was painted with a willow-pattern type motif. I understand that they still have similar contraptions in Buckingham Palace. I cannot think what came over my grandfather to allow such a modern feature to be installed.

La Houguette, as this house was called, was a most imposing mansion built of grey Jersey granite. One approached it by a circular carriage drive which swept around a central lawn, in the middle of which stood an immense monkey-puzzle tree. This tree was the pride and joy of my grandfather's heart. Flanking the drive on the other side was a positive wall of beautiful camellias. They were in all colours, pinks and red, striped and white. They were glorious when in flower.

Two elegant flights of steps upwards in a graceful curve to the front door. This led into an immense entrance hall, with two very large rooms on each side.

On the left were the back and front drawing-rooms. These were never used in my time. They were packed full of hideous Victoriana which would be priceless today. I think it was all thrown away when my grandfather died.

On the opposite side of the hall there was a comfortable living-room which they used for all purposes and behind that was a library which was largely filled with books about Napoleon, for whom my grandfather had a great admiration.

There was a door at the rear of the hall which led to a fantastic feature. The stairs leading down to the kitchen premises were pitch dark. But there was a glimmer of light once one had the courage to start descending, as the risers, behind the treads, were ingeniously made of

My mother, about 1910.

My Jersey Grandfather.

glass. The aunts belted up and down this staircase with the speed of long familiarity. My sister and I found it very creepy.

The ground floor was a warren of little rooms leading off about an acre of stone-flagged passage. I cannot think how the aunts coped.

There were several handsome bedrooms on the upper floor and another warren of attics. If this was not enough there was a glass structure erected over all called the "look-out" where, I seem to remember, the aunts dried the washing in wet weather.

On each end of the main house there were two little wings that had been built as dower houses, where I suppose unwanted elderly members of the family could be banished if need be. I always felt that these little dower houses were the most attractive features of the whole place. The rooms were sensibly proportioned and always seemed to be sunny and bright. They were unfurnished when we knew them and the aunts stored apples in them, and they smelled deliciously of these and of wood smoke.

The gardens were pleasant but neglected. The tennis lawn was covered with primroses. Behind the house were terraced gardens where I can remember picking enormous rasberries and redcurrants, sun-warmed against the old granite walls. There was a stable yard and outbuildings where Aunty May kept her poultry.

My grandfather did not approve of Daylight Saving, as British Summer Time used to be called, first introduced, I think, during the 1914-1918 war. He simply ignored it and when he was sitting on the bench (he was stipendiary magistrate with the title of Judge), people had to work out what time it really was, Judge Vaudin's time or B.S.T.

He bore a striking resemblance to the Archduke of Austria. In about 1900, he was travelling in Austria and was once mistaken for the Archduke. The guard was turned out in a hurry to salute him when he was passing the palace. I bet he enjoyed that.

He had another idiosyncrasy that used to demoralise us as children. We had no car until I was in my teens, so when we went to see my grandparents on a Sunday afternoon we either walked or took the bus. If grandfather took it into his head to come and meet us, he would insist on us all walking in step. It drove him mad to see anyone out of step. But how in the world could small girls keep pace for pace with a very tall old gentleman? Sometimes he gave us "more in sorrow than in anger" looks, and blamed my father for not bringing us up properly!

My grandmother became an invalid the year I was born in 1917. I only remember her as a pretty little white-haired old lady, sitting in an armchair by the fire in winter and by the window in summer.

For about twenty years the three aunts worked on an elaborate rota of duties. Only two of them were ever out together. As the years went by and both old people needed more attention, they reversed this and two of them were always at home whilst the other went out.

The youngest sister, my Auntie Stella, broke out against stern parental opposition and bought a little bull-nosed Morris car. Somewhat to our awe, my father and his sisters called their parents, Pater and Mater. This is about the sum total of my knowledge of Latin. Anyway, this little car was bought to take Pater out. They had to disconnect the speedometer as he kept his eyes glued to the dial and never stopped ordering her to slow down.

They had a puncture one day and Aunty Stella went to a nearby house to telephone for help. My grandfather was so much struck by this, he went straight down to see my father.

"I want one of those instruments, Sonny," he told father, who must have been well over forty at the time. He could not think what the old gentleman meant but did manage to elucidate his meaning after a while.

My mother said, "Get the gas and electricity in at the same time whilst he's in the mood." But this was going too far. My mother worried about the aunts having so few comforts but at least they no longer had to run over a mile to the nearest phone.

My grandfather never minded telling a story against himself. I remember my father repeating the following little tale as told him by Pater.

"I felt like a bus ride," pater said with a twinkle in his eye. "I sat down by a lady and naturally I started telling her about Jersey as I thought she was a visitor. I told her about how we always tethered our cows, and I pointed out the piles of vraic (seaweed) we used to manure the ground. I explained how all the southern slopes were cultivated for the early potatoes and that these fields were called cotils, and of course, I mentioned all the places of interest as we passed them. And do you know, Sonny, when we got out of the bus she shook my hand and said 'Thank you, Judge Vaudin.' She was a Jersey lady all the time."

As my grandfather dearly loved his island I imagine he talked non-stop. Everything was of interest to him and he felt he must share it. He was over eighty when he stopped going on his little bus rides.

My mother was English and I think for a long time she was treated by her in-laws as something of a foreigner. Her father was also a gentleman of great character.

He was a corn and seed merchant and much enjoyed a running battle with Stanley Baldwin when he was in iower, to do more for the farmers and the agricultural industry in general. Mr. Baldwin was a native of Bewdley where he had his home right up until his death. Bewdley was just next door to Kidderminster where my grandfather Dalley had his business.

He was a pioneer in the sugar beet industry in this country. He married twice, and managed to have a silver wedding with each lady, which was pretty smart of him.

My mother was the eldest child of the first family. My grandmother, who not surprisingly died in her early forties, had four children under five. My Uncle Reg, who was the youngest child of the first family, was the Dalley part of the famous firm of estate agents, Doolittle and Dalley. The firm still exists but alas there are no more Doolittles or Dalleys left but I do not blame them for keeping up that delightful name.

It was when my mother's stepmother started the second family, that she decided to take off for Russia. She had been engaged for seven years to someone who was working in India and not surprisingly, after all that time, she got fed up and broke it off. She and her two sisters were most beautiful girls and never lacked for admirers. Little Brother Reg used to cash in, accepting tips from their young men, to keep father away. He was a terrific martinet when it came to his daughters' suitors.

But talking of martinets I must refer again to my Jersey grandfather. When I was about eight years old, he made an unannounced state call on us when I was alone in the house in the charge of a young French maid. We were both appalled, but made a valiant effort to produce tea and cakes and I did my poor best, shaking in my shoes, to entertain him.

When he left, he gravely shook my hand, we were never on more familiar terms, and said, "It's a pity your mother can't afford to buy you some stockings and a proper skirt to hide your legs!" I was so dashed, as I thought my short socks and gym tunic were quite in order for a little girl. What the poor gentleman would say if he could see a bikini, does not bear thinking about.

I loved school. I was a poor sportswoman and mediocre scholar, but I tried. I did manage to get into the Junior School netball team, but damaged my ankle rather badly just before the annual inter-insular fixture with Guernsey Ladies' College, which was *the* sporting event of the entire school year. I must say I was very upset at having to drop out of the team at the last minute.

There were two of us in my form who could not sing. I do think this is something one cannot learn. I can remember Mr. May, the singing master, looking at Palma and myself as if we were something that had crept out of the woodwork.

"It isn't possible," he kept saying. "Not two of them. It can't be true. It just isn't possible." We were a sad trial to him.

Academically, I was quite good at History and English, half-hearted about the sciences, mildly interested in foreign languages and downright hopeless at maths and art. It must have been sickening for my father who had a magnificent brain for figures, and who was appointed one of the youngest bank managers ever known. He was also almost unique in that he went into the Jersey branch of Lloyds Bank as junior clerk, "washing inkpots" as he used to tell us, and finished up as

My father's home, "Le Houguette" Jersey; now a boys school.

manager in the same branch without ever having had a move. His flair for figures showed when he played bridge, which game he played exceptionally well.

I never learnt to sew because I deliberately lost every piece of needlework issued to me.

Up would go my hand. "Please, may I read aloud?" "Can I read *The Secret Garden* this term?" "We finished the *Water Babies* last term," or "What about *Little Lord Fauntleroy*?"

Again I cannot think what the teacher was about to let me do this term after term. I liked reading aloud to the others and I dare say she thought I was unteachable. In my reports she used to say my needlework was "not up to standard". As I never even threaded a needle, this was surely the understatement of all time.

Leaving the island for our summer holidays was always both dramatic and traumatic. My mother started feeling seasick in the steamship office when she went to book our tickets. There was a churchyard right opposite the office and she used to pace round there amongst the tombstones with a hankie pressed to her mouth. I was brought to England in 1919 when I was two, but I can not pretend to remember anything about that trip. My mother flatly refused to travel alone with us two children, so elaborate arrangements had to be made for my father to accompany us on the outward journey and to fetch us back at the end of the holiday. When we visited mother's family in England, it was quite a prolonged affair. Alternate years we went to France on a much briefer trip.

The boats that ran to France were terrible, but it was only a three-hour crossing. They were very small boats and had no decent accommodation at all. Well, none suitable for seasick ladies with seasick children. The boats that came to England were bigger and better but of course stabilizers had not been thought of, and the crossing from the Channel Islands is notorious for its unpleasantness. My mother and I were both frightful sailors, my sister was a bit better, and as long as father had to look after us, he seemed to be a very good traveller. It was so odd that when Roselle and I were big enough to look after ourselves, he started to succumb too. I have the liveliest recollection of a square sort of room lined with tiers of bunks which rejoiced in the name of the ladies saloon. A starched and crackling lady would be hovering, ever ready to remove our basins, poor soul. There was no air service until about 1933, I think. Then they were little eight-seater planes, landing

My grandfather on the bench; Jersey.

and taking off from the sands, when the tide happened to be right.

There is one journey I shall always regret having missed. My sister went to school in Switzerland for a year. When my parents took her there, I was left behind in England with an aunt. Fond of my aunt though I was, I thought very poorly at being abandoned by my whole family in one fell swoop. I was twelve at the time.

When they were passing through the customs at St. Malo, Roselle's trunk was opened by the douanne. The officer prodded about amongst her things and eventually raised aloft a large box of sanitary towels, demanding loudly "Qu'est-ce que c'est?"

My mother was so embarrassed and enraged that she did her best to make him put them down by hitting at his arm. With tears of laughter pouring down her cheeks she has told me the story so often. "And your father," she said, "just stood there, raising his hat!"

He had no idea what the fuss was about but was convinced my mother would be hurled into gaol for striking a custom's official. *Toujours la politesse*, he hoped to placate authority with his exquisite good manners!

There used to be the most charming little railways in Jersey years ago. They were real passenger trains running on a narrow gauge single track. There were no corridor carriages of course. One line ran east and was closed in 1929. The other line lasted a little longer. The other line ran west and south, and actually went through a real tunnel. I suppose the tunnel was only a few yards long in reality, but to us it seemed as long as a possible channel tunnel. There were no refinements like lights in the carriages so it was with delicious terror we would plunge into darkness. If we had forgotten to close the window, we would be even more delighted with the smoke, smuts and smells that poured in.

It was said that when a rather unhappy Prince of Wales visited Jersey just before his father died, the sight of our toy-town trains was the only thing that made him smile.

A famous personality I remember seeing from time to time when I was young was Sir Jesse Boot, later Lord Trent, who was the founder of Boots the Cash Chemists in Nottingham.

He married a Jersey lady, Miss Rowe, whose father kept a newspaper and tobacconist shop in St. Helier.

He was a great benefactor both to Jersey and Nottingham. When I remember him he was a helpless invalid, which was so sad. Even millionaires cannot buy health. We used to see him being driven round,

My grandparents, parents and three aunts and Roselle my sister about 1915.

taking the air, in a special chair that was hoisted into a specially-built car. I was told he only had sufficient movement in one hand to press a bell attached to his chest. His brain was astonishingly active and he kept numerous secretaries working round the clock to keep pace with his fertile plans.

Later in my life I recall my father telling me that when Lady Trent visited the bank, he was summoned out to the car to sit with her whilst she transacted her business. I gathered that, at this time, she was in no way incapacitated, and though the words were not spoken, I got the impression that my father thought poorly of this manoeuvre.

I remember when Lily Langtry died, she was buried in St. Saviour's churchyard not far from my grandparents.

As my father's sisters did not marry, we had no Jersey cousins. However, we did have three boy cousins who lived in Kidderminster. If we were not visiting them, they spent many summer holidays with us.

The eldest boy was nine years older than me. Though he teased me unmercifully, I was devoted to him. He would sometimes kindly do my arithmetic homework for me. This nearly drove me mad when the problems would be about trains rushing in different directions, or men digging holes or taps filling baths with water. Basil would look over my shoulder when I was struggling with a mass of figures and say, "The answer's ten, of course," or whatever it was.

This would cause me to wail, "I can't just put the answer down. I have to show the workings," which would send him off into a fit of laughter. As far as he was concerned, the problem was so simple there were no workings to show. It may have been obvious to a great man of eighteen, but to a dim-witted little girl, nothing was obvious or simple.

Basil once plagued me so much that I hit him with my skipping-rope and every time I happened to glance at him for the rest of his holiday, he had one eye shut. I had caught him a fleeting blow over his eyebrow with my wild hit, but not hurt him in the least. But he made me think I had damaged his eye, and I was so fond of him, I cried myself to sleep for nights. How he roared with laughter when I told him this years later.

Once, when he was staying with us, I happened to have a birthday. I think I must have reached "double figures" so it was a special birthday. My parents hired a small bus and we took about twenty little girls, plus Basil, for a picnic on the beach. He was so good with all these children that they all fell in love with him and fought like tigers to sit next to him in the bus going home. I still have a photograph of this outing.

Aubrey was the cousin next in age. He once held me over a bonfire till my panties scorched. I went in howling to my aunt, Aubrey's mother, who said, "It's your own fault for playing with him." Aunty Ede never did have much time for her own sex!

My youngest cousin, Rex, was about two years older than me, and we once had an adventure that kept us laughing for years.

We had decided to walk out at low tide to a castle in the middle of St. Aubin's Bay, spend the day there, and walk back again at night, when the tide had gone down again, and the causeway was once more negotiable. Unfortunately, we had miscalculated the times of the tide, and when we arrived on the beach in the morning, the causeway was covered.

Unwilling to be beaten by anything so trivial as a brisk in-coming tide, we persuaded the bathing machine man, called Mr. Fry, to lend us his boat, plus an ancient and diminutive man. This worthy, and his even older boat, were accustomed to paddle gently round the sea water bathing-pool which was used at low tide.

Why Mr. Fry always insisted that our cousins were our brothers I have no idea, but he always called Rex "Mr. Vaudin", even when he was about twelve.

Anyway, we eventually set off in this boat and it seemed that the wind sprung up immediately, and of course we were rowing against the

My Aunt Stella in the Bull-Nosed Morris, 1920s.

tide. The old boat was unused to such cavalier treatment and began to leak, or maybe it was the wavelets splashing over the side, but I know we began to get very wet. Rex and the ancient ordered me to bale for my life. They each had an oar, and the rowlocks kept coming adrift, causing the ancient to fall over backwards.

Mr. Fry kept leaping about on the water's edge yelling, "Let Mr. Vaudin row," which, had we not been so occupied, would have made us fall out of the boat with laughter. The language coming from that poor little man was new to me, too!

We did arrive eventually at the castle after quite a hazardous trip and all three of us were soaked. We gave the old chap all the money we had on us. I do not think we could have raised more than a couple of shillings between us, as we did not have a lot of pocket-money. I think his journey back was not quite so hair-raising as the tide would have helped him. I am quite sure if my parents had seen us setting off we would have been unceremoniously hauled back.

My mother always wished she could swim and she made sure we could. When we were tiny she would spend hours in the water up to her knees holding us up and encouraging us. We never had water-wings or armbands such as I see children have today. Undressing on the beach in all weathers, we soon learnt to get on with it.

She was also anxious that we should speak French. My sister's French is good because she spent a year in Switzerland. I picked up my conversational French from Bretonne maids, and, according to my Parisian cousin, my accent is "formidable".

I think we had a sheltered childhood. I was in my early teens when my Jersey grandmother died, and, thankfully, I was not taken to the funeral. I did go to my grandfathers however, a few years later. Predictably, he took his last journey in a horse-drawn hearse followed by carriages, though motorised funeral processions had been in the island for some time. One of my mother's brothers was posted "missing believed killed" in 1917. For years my mother believed he would return. He was with the Canadians at Vimy Ridge.

Our parents' conversation was continually referring nostalgically to the magic days "before the war".

Little did we think in the safe, happy childhood of the 1920s that in less than two decades we should be in the middle of another war.

How often I have heard myself boring the younger generation with those self-same words "before the war".

HOLIDAY TIME

My sister and I 1927, Fliquet.

Seaside holidays.

CHAPTER TWO

Georgian Summer 1934-1940

The last holiday we had together as a family was a cruise to Norway. I think it was 1930. The recession was beginning and the Cunard Company had transfered one of their smaller liners to the Norwegian fjords for a season.

I really do not know how my father managed to persuade mother to embark on such an adventure when she was such a poor sailor. Mercifully, my sister and I were in our teens and, in theory, self-sufficient. I remember I was awfully seasick in the North Sea, but I think I was the only one of us to succumb on this occasion, because, as I recall, I *would* get up and go on deck, whilst the rest of the family stayed quietly in their cabins. Also, by this time, we had discovered some new wonder seasick remedy which helped. We did not collapse, wholesale in heaps, quite so constantly.

When we went to Norway, my father informed us in an aghast voice, "I have *never* spent so much on a holiday in my life! Do you know we are paying £1 a day *each*? Even for you," he added, glancing at me.

We were duly impressed and made sure we should enjoy our holiday to the full. It was a grand cruise and I shall always remember Norway as a bright, colourful, very clean place.

We went overland to a glacier miles from anywhere, and a beautiful blonde Norwegian girl was selling handknitted scarves, one of which I instantly craved. I only had English money, but I hopefully held up half-a-crown.

"That," she said in crisp, faultless English, "Is approximately correct!" I was quite overcome between shame and admiration. We British never seem to try and learn any other language, do we? Maybe we do nowadays. We certainly did not then.

One of the reasons we abruptly stopped taking family holidays was the Dominion of the Cats. We were all very fond of our two cats. Minnie Tarah—a very ordinary tabby with white shoes and socks and a white shirt-front—grew up with us. I was about five when she came to us as a kitten, and she had to be put down after I had gone to college when I was seventeen.

Her daughter was called Yvonne Tissionaire! I cannot imagine how they came to acquire such names nor do I know how to spell them. Yvonne was just like her mum, and they were really remarkably intelligent and lovable. What is more, they ruled the house.

We used to ask neighbours to feed them when we were away and we left beds for them in the outhouses. It was very difficult packing a suitcase as they knew the signs and kept trying to climb into the cases so that they would not be left behind. Someone told us how they pined. That did it. In a body, with one voice, we decreed "No more family holidays. We'll go away in turns," and so we did, ever after. Someone was always at home to look after the cats!

My father contemplated, at one time, taking out health insurance policies for us all but decided against it as we all seemed so healthy. Within a very few years, my mother, Roselle and myself all had appendicitis. My mother was very ill, but I was never sure whether I really had it or not. One's appendix used to be whipped out at the drop of a hat in those days and one would be kept in bed for ten days. We all went to a very comfortable and I am afraid expensive, nursing home.

My mother was just recovering from this when we went to Norway and that next winter father went down with pneumonia. It was at Christmas-time, and there were no antibiotics then. We had to wait for the "crisis", to know if he was going to live or die. He never really fully recovered from this and he was prone to bronchitis and asthma for the rest of his life. I think perhaps I began to grow up a little, what with mother's appendix and father's pneumonia.

I was in Devonshire with my father on one of our staggered holidays when the School Leaving Certificate results came out. I suppose in modern terms it was "O" levels. I managed a distinction in History and mercifully, in French. Had I failed in French, I should never have dared to return to Jersey, because the teacher, a Jersey lady, was so terrifying. We learnt from sheer fear. She had spent her whole life at the Jersey Ladies' College, first as a pupil, then as a teacher. Years later, when this really lovely lady, who was a superb teacher and

The library, University of Reading.

disciplinarian, retired, she was invited by the English branch of the Old Girls' Association to a presentation ceremony in London.

The chairman, addressing an audience that varied in age from seventeen to seventy, began by saying, "Everyone of us in this room has suffered from Miss Holt." It was impossible for her to continue for some minutes, so great was the laughter and the applause. Miss Holt, now nicely mellowed with years, laughed more than anyone. As I write she is in her 97th year. Her brain is as clear and her speech as crisp and concise as it ever was.

Miss Holt, I salute you!

I think I have always been something of a hoarder. I love cardboard boxes and pieces of string and photographs and old letters and newspaper cuttings. It really pains me to throw away last year's Christmas cards! Every year or two I have a little blitz and throw away everything then spend some weeks regretting it. One thing I am very glad I have kept is my mother's passport to Russia in 1910.

I do not think that, prior to 1914, passports were in general use, so

Clock Tower, University of Reading.

this document is quite interesting. It is rather like a sheet of parchment with a beautiful coat of arms, signed by Sir Edward Grey with his own hand, and graced with a sixpenny stamp.

I have also clung to favourite childhood books, Beatrix Potter, Arthur Mee's *Hero Book* (the only prize I ever won) and *Verses for Children*, exquisitely illustrated by Margaret Tarrant.

When I was seven, we had a holiday at a convent at St. Servan, in Brittany. It seemed strange but it was ideal for children. There were very extensive grounds, a private beach, and hordes of French children to play with. The only other English child was a small boy, who was the son of the Professor of Dairying at Reading University.

Precocious brat that I must have been, I announced to this gentleman that I was coming to his college one day to learn gardening. I did, too, and the Todds were still there and were most kind to me.

I arrived in Reading to take a two-year Diploma Course in Horticulture in 1934. I enjoyed my training immensely, though it was a cruel shock to find that geometry figured in surveying when we came to calculate the area of a circular lawn or pond.

Never having been away from home before, I felt quite abandoned. My poor father took me to Reading and left me there in tears and went on to see my sister who had just started training as a Nurse in Birmingham. He found her also in tears because she was so pleased to see him. He must have had a terrible time between the pair of us.

He was a rather retiring man, incredibly tolerant and with a marvellous dry sense of humour. I think he was the most conscientous man I have ever known. His staff at the bank, often told me in later years, that he was held in high esteem because he was totally just and fair. His insistence on seeing both sides of every question tried my patience beyond bearing during the war.

He had a very sharp eye for a forger and I can remember him rumbling one. The only way people could leave the Island in those days was by boat and my father went down to the pier each morning with the police.

When he came back one morning he was very depressed. "I'd made up my mind that if the chap didn't show up this morning I would give up," he said. "But I spotted him and how I wish I hadn't. He had his wife and child with him and she was so upset. It was dreadful. I wish he'd got away now. After all, he didn't get the money because I spotted it when he tried it on."

Even when I was a child I felt I could predict his reactions to almost anything, but in this I was sometimes quite wrong.

For instance, my parents were contemplating moving to a larger house. My mother held the belief that one should move every ten years. She much enjoyed organising removals. We were all rather thrilled and excited about moving to this much nicer house, then father decided, after further consideration, against it, for economic reasons.

I thought the matter was closed, and I do not know why because it was not all that important, but I shed a mild tear or two from disappointment. To my amazement, he got up at once, went straight to the telephone and bought the new house on the spot. It was on that day I discovered that my father could not bear to see a woman cry. I was about eleven, but to do my sister and I justice, we never traded on our discovery.

Another time he surprised me was when, years after the event, we were discussing the visit of the King and Queen in 1921. My parents had been invited to a garden party to meet the royal couple.

"What were they really like, close to?" I asked him. "I wish I could have been there too."

"I have no idea," he replied, "They were so awe inspiring and majestic and everything was on such a scale of grandeur, I just closed my eyes and bowed!"

My parents were devoted to each other and never argued. If they did not just see eye to eye on any rare occasion, my father brought the subject to a close by saying, "I agree with you, my dear, but I think differently." One has to admit it was diplomatic, unanswerable and maddening!

My mother was a splendid mother but the children came a long way behind my Father in importance in her eyes, which we appreciated and understood. My cousin, Mary, for whom these reminiscences are written, has said to me more than once that the only two perfect marriages she has ever heard of, are her parents and mine. Mary was born in 1935 so does not figure in my real childhood memories. I am eighteen years older than she, and I am eighteen years younger than her mother. I am sure a numerologist would find something of significance in this. I can only say that all three of us are very good friends.

Such was my mother's enthusiasm for us to learn French, all the cleaning ladies, besides the maid, were usually Bretonne. I remember one dear lady who used a totally unique language entirely her own. She could neither read or write. I have treasured her remarks for many years. One of the best was when I said to her one day, "Are you going to wait for the bus, Mde Helleur?" and she replied, "Je ne stoperay par pour it!"

This same cleaning lady was a sad trial to us at one period because she was so totally emotionally uncontrolled and tender-hearted. My mother's sister had a tragic car accident when her husband was killed when she was driving. Aunty Edith came to stay with us for a long visit to recover from the accident. Whenever Mde Helleur caught sight of my aunt, the good lady burst into tears, and fled, sobbing in some disorder. There was no stopping her. It was very upsetting for everyone.

In a fit of mental aberration, one day, my mother became so confused with all these French-speaking people around her, she decided that *everyone* must be French and proceeded accordingly.

There was a little Yorkshireman working in the house at the time, doing some painting. He was quietly lifting the stair-carpet in preparation to paint the staircase. My mother decided he should have a box in which to put the nails he was taking out of the stair-carpet. To address a foreigner, you must know, one has to shout. To attract his attention she dealt him a blow on the arm and shouted, "A boyte? Vous voulez a *boyte*?" The poor little man shot her a terrified look and scuttled down the stairs to find my father.

"I don't know what Mrs. Vaudin wants," he said to my father. "I think she is speaking to me in a foreign language."

My father finished filling his pipe, he was a deliberate man, and strolled upstairs to find Mother had shut herself up in the bathroom and given way to hysterical laughter.

Another time, my mother was opening a bottle of vinegar and a drop or two somehow splashed into her eye. This caused her some degree of pain. We had a Jersey maid at this time, called Doris, who was hovering anxiously about when my father appeared and was told what had happened. Strolling on, he remarked, "I hope you have not wasted much!"

Doris was so thunderstruck by the apparent callousness of this remark that she gasped out; "Well, I'm damned!"

I do not know how I have started all these stories about my parents because I set out to write about my next step into the great waiting world at Reading.

My sister in nursing uniform with myself in gardening uniform for Reading University, 1934.

As a student at Reading 1935. Academic dress.

Myself, Guernsey 1938.

The horticultural students had to give up part of every vacation to stay on at the university and do practical work. We very much enjoyed this because there were so few of us, and rules were relaxed. Also, at the very beginning, when as a Fresher, it was good to be able to get your bearings before all the hordes of other students arrived.

I made friends the very first day with Jean Thompson. There is an old popular song called *I hear music when I think of you*. Well, I hear laughter when I think of Jean. We laughed our way through every minute of our two years. I knew I had to share a bedroom for the first year and I was dreading this. I had shared Roselle's room when very young, but at an early age had begged for my own room. I went up to the attic, next to the box-room. There was no gaslighting up there, we did not have electric light until the next move, so I had to have a candle or paraffin lamp in the winter. Looking back, I cannot imagine how my careful parents allowed it.

So I had a good long look at Jean, and asked her if she would like to share with me. She had been having a good look at me with the same idea, and that day a lifelong friendship was born. She married a G.I. and went to the States in 1946. She had a pretty tough time out there but has two super sons that make up for everything, though she was always homesick for England. We obviously do not meet very often. But when we do, we take up exactly where we left off.

I saw fit to fall in love during my first term with the biggest fish in our little pool, the president of the Students' Union, no less. I am absolutely certain, that he was never aware even of my existence. That did not matter in the least. I was content to worship from afar.

Jean fell in and out of love constantly. We were both sufficiently well-balanced to know it was all growing pains and enjoyed ourselves immensely through it all.

We liked the practical work best. We spent three days a week at the horticultural station, and the other three days having lectures at the university. Apart from all the branches of pure horticulture, we had lectures in botany, chemistry, physics, soil chemistry, entomology, plant physiology, microbiology, mycology, rural economics and surveying. We both finished up with second class passes with which we were quite satisfied as girls *never* got firsts. There were twenty-one of us in our year, fourteen boys and seven girls.

In rural economics, a subject in which I did not shine, we had to study in depth the workings of the first horticultural co-operative society in the country. This was in 1934. I was quite amazed, when, in 1974, chance brought me to live in Badsey, forty years later, where the Littleton and Badsey Growers' Association, whose function I had studied with such pain, was only just up the road from my house and still very much in business.

We had to cycle three miles to the horticultural station, up the main Basingstoke Road. That was another thing, I had never cycled, let alone owned a bike.

My father bought me the very best bicycle he could. It was a B.S.A. and cost £7. He came out with me once or twice but my wobbling about so unnerved him, I got on better by myself. I sold it when we left Jersey in 1945 for £20. It had served me very faithfully for years.

The summer of 1935 was a beautiful hot summer. It was the year of King George V's Silver Jubilee. A friend of mine once said later that the King's jubilee year was the last happy and peaceful time Britain was ever to know. I think she might have been right.

I was ill during my first term at Reading. To this day I do not know what ailed me. It taught me one good thing. I have ever since had a profound respect and admiration for lady doctors. Hitherto, with the indifference of youth, I scarcely knew they existed, and, had I thought about them at all, I would have dismissed them as inconsequential.

I had a temperature and appalling headaches for what seemed like weeks. Before I was sent up to the university sanatorium I was in bed at the hall of residence. Jean was away working at the horticultural station and I never saw a soul all day. I had such pain in my head that I thought I had three heads and got quite worked up because I only had two hands with which to clutch them!

At the sanatorium I was tended by two aged ladies, trained nurses both. As a seventeen-year-old, I took their joint ages to be about 200 years. I dare say they were in their fifties. They nearly drove me mad by persisting in talking baby-talk to me. "Shallus clean our toosie-pegs den?" for example or possibly, "Is oo ready for din-dins?"

For some reason best known to my medical attendants (they produced specialists, too) I was kept in purdah. Jean was not allowed to come near me. I never knew why. I doubt I would have survived without Dr. Field's daily visit. She did provide some sane conversation and I liked her immensely.

My aunt came down from Kidderminster to see me, and then my sister came from her training hospital in Birmingham. These visits began to frighten me. I felt I must surely be at death's door to warrant all this attention. My poor mother telephoned constantly from Jersey; she did not know what to think as I kept insisting I was all right. She was unable to come and see for herself because my father was not very well. It was mid-winter, just before Christmas, and the seas at that particular time were mountainous. The mail boats were running late or not at all. Much as I would have loved to see her, I could not bear the thought of her sufferings, had she embarked on the journey.

I was sent up to my long-suffering aunt in Kidderminster because they would not let me go home for Christmas. This was a real blow and I must say I was very upset at not going home for my first holidays. Things worked out all right, of course, as they usually do, but when one is young and not feeling very well, it is hard to be philosophical.

During the long hot summer of the Jubilee, Jean made me go swimming with her in the Thames at Sonning. We found a place, bordering a cornfield, which had a sandy bottom, because I refused to wade through mud. Jean had quite a time getting me to go in, because it was so different from the sea and the beaches to which I was accustomed.

We cycled everywhere, which was quite hazardous in the town of Reading because if one got caught up in the tramlines one skidded along out of control.

As I could not go home to Jersey for half-terms, Jean's parents often asked me to stay with them. They had a most beautiful big house with a perfect garden in Northamptonshire. I did enjoy staying with them.

Jean came twice to Jersey. She spent a long visit the summer before the war when we had a most glorious free time. My parents were in France for a month at Mont D'or. My father was there to take a course of treatment in the clean mountain air for his asthma and bronchitis.

Jean and I were very keen on surfing, so we arranged our lives around the tides, because the surf was better on an incoming tide. I do not think we did any housework and only washed up when there was no crockery left from which to eat. It is good to think we had such a splendid carefree time before our world fell into bits around us.

I often wonder what happened to the avenue of peach trees we grew when we were at Reading. My Jersey grandfather, at the turn of the century, had purchased a most delicious peach in St. Malo. He was so impressed with the flavour, he carefully took the stone home and planted it in his garden.

In 1912, when my mother married father, the peach tree was as high as a house, and the aunts were picking the fruit in washing-baskets. In her turn, my mother was impressed and sent stones back to England. During my years at Reading we raised a lot of seedlings. It was called Peche Vaudin or the Jersey Peach. There was no need to bother with grafting or budding, training, or indeed pruning. I have the same strain still and pick quantities of fruit in late September provided the weather is right. The blossom is pretty too which is another bonus. Being early flowering there is always a risk of late frosts, but as long as the tree is given water in abundance during spring and summer, even peach leaf curl seems to be controlled.

Owing to my slight stammer and difficulty with Rs, travelling alone to Reading by train was something of a nightmare, I found it so awkward to ask porters and ticket collectors for the right platform. The more I thought about it the worse it became. What torments youth can suffer.

Like Maurice Chevalier, "I'm glad I'm not young any more." Jean and I used to go up to London sometimes to see a play or window shop. It would not have occurred to either of us to start out with out hats and gloves! I had £52 a year dress allowance from my father, paid half-yearly. Jean had £6 a month so at the end of every six months we were broke together.

A member of father's staff at the bank was moved to London for head office training. He was very homesick for Jersey in the early days. "I go rowing on the Serpentine," he once told me. "It's the nearest I can get to the sea."

Jean and I used to meet him sometimes and he was very kind to a couple of giggly teenagers. Derek was nine years older than I, and as long as I can remember, he was on hand at children's Christmas parties and he took me to my first dances. He married a very musical lady eventually, and their daughter is Jaqueline Du Pre, the celebrated but unfortunate cellist.

Once, when Jean was coming back to Jersey with me, we stayed a night at the Strand Palace Hotel. Bed and breakfast at the time was 8/6d. Jean was not at all sure whether it was quite respectable. I was too simple to know what she meant. In fact, I owe Jean a great debt of gratitude as she was good enough to inform me about the facts of life! At seventeen, I had not a clue. I shall never forget how she laughed. I dare say I should *never* have known if it had not been for Jean!

Some years later I came across a young girl called Clarice Mary Alice.

If this was not funny enough she eventually married a Mr. Harris. At eighteen years old, she was informed by me of the facts of life. I laughed immoderately because I kept remembering how Jean laughed at me. I never dreamed I would meet anybody as innocent as myself.

When we came down from Reading, Jean obtained a job at an alpine flower nursery and had an interesting time because her firm had stands at all the big flower shows all over the country. Just before the war she went to work at Kew Gardens, and was there for the duration. At the time of the V-bombs she was working in the glasshouses, growing fruit for Great Ormond Street Hospital for Sick Children. It must have been a terrible nervous strain working under glass with those buzz-bombs cutting out overhead.

Before the end of the war she married a G.I. and her first baby was born in England, and later with other G.I. brides was taken back to the States in 1946. She once told me it was a nightmare journey.

I got a job in Jersey. I had promised my parents I would stay at home for a year or two. The two women I worked for were quite unbelievable. Looking back, I really cannot understand how my parents let me join them. I think they must have been lesbians, but I dare say my parents did not know about such things in those days. I certainly did not. It is only recently that this thought has occurred to me, when I started to think about how peculiar they were.

They taught me one thing for which I shall always be grateful. I learned to keep my temper under severe provocation. Though I do think the good fairies at my christening had something to do with it, too, because if I am roused I am immediately struck dumb. It is impossible to answer back when you are deprived of the power of speech. This gift has stood me in very good stead.

I bought a Morris two-seater with a dickey for £10. It was not the bull-nosed variety but the next model. In this I went to work and carried one or other of my employers around. Prior to my arrival, one walked and the other cycled. They ran a jolly good little business. Firstly, it was an agency for supplying jobbing gardeners by the day on demand. They employed about a dozen men. Anyone who wanted it, could hire a skilled man to do a day's pruning, or if they owned big gardens, they could contract to have a man two or three days a week on a regular basis. Secondly, they rented pockets of land all over the island and there they grew all manner of crops which they sold in two shops in the town, which they also ran.

They paid me eightpence an hour when it was fine. If it rained I went home with no pay. I have never really mastered my eight-times table so this was an added irritation! After a prolonged fine spell I would find myself praying for rain to have a short rest, and of course, conversely, when it rained for days together, I would long for it to stop so that I could earn a few bob. I cannot remember what arrangement we made about the car. Petrol at that time in Jersey was tenpence-halfpenny a gallon.

With my first week's money I took my mother out to tea at a very nice tea shop called Gaudins, which I am happy to say is one of the few places in Jersey that has not changed with the passing years.

I was at home for the abdication crisis in 1936, which came as a tremendous shock. I know now that some people had seen American and Continental papers that were full of the unhappy news, but the British Press had been magnificently silent on the subject and we had not the slightest idea that anything was wrong. Feelings ran so high one had an uneasy impression that Britain might be on the verge of civil war. Even my ever-tolerant father spoke up quite sharply against Mrs. Simpson. All our hearts went out to the Duke of York who must have been daunted at the prospect of stepping out of comparative peace and obscurity, into the full glaring limelight of the throne.

I went to George VI's coronation the following year. An aunt and I had seats over Carrington the Jewellers in Regent Street.

We were staying in Sussex and went up to London by train the evening before. I suppose we must have wandered about all night, but I have no very clear recollection of any of it. It was all so tiring and of course I started one of my headaches! One might have known. It rained I remember, because when we came out into Regent Street when it was all over, we had to wade through sodden newspapers about a yard deep.

In some ways I am like my grandfather Vaudin in that I do not care much for so-called progress, but I do think television is wonderful, especially for royal occasions!

Sometime before my sister and I left the island in 1934, my parents built themselves a little bungalow of Canadian cedar. It consisted of one very large room, a kitchen and loo. There were also two balconies, one each side. This little house was a lasting source of pleasure to all of us and our visitors from England. It was built practically on the beach where we went surfing. My mother carved the name of her doll's house with her own hands, "Roma". It had nothing to do with Italy but stood for Rodney and Mary (my parents), and Roselle and Margaret (my sister and I).

It was a trifle primitive, perhaps. We cooked with paraffin and we went there in all weathers. I particularly recall with pleasure many a Boxing Day treat, when we went to Roma with with our drumsticks and mince pies. We could sleep four in comparative comfort, two in the main room and one on each of the balconies, and everyone thought it was heaven. The Germans blew it up in 1944.

During the winter of 1937, when I was twenty, I had decided that I would like to specialise in flower production and/or bulb production. I thought Holland would be a good place to start, and tentatively brought up the subject with my parents.

They raised hands of horror. Hitler was ranting on about his territorial demands and everyone was talking about the war that was surely coming. I never bothered to think very much about this. I had read books like *All quiet on the Western Front* and seen *Journey's End* at the theatre, and I could not imagine how such terrible things could possibly be allowed to happen again. It was not twenty years since the last war had ended.

So my parents said "No" with one voice to my idea of working on the Continent. I was a bit dashed as I thought it would have been very interesting. I had another think and told them perhaps I should try the Scilly Isles.

This idea caused my mother to turn quite pale and say in a failing voice, "Two seas to cross! However should I get to you if you were ill? You can't really want to go to the Scilly Isles."

My father was quietly reading his newspaper and put it down long enough to say, "Why don't you go to Guernsey?"

I don't remember ever being so affronted. It was like living in Brighton and going to work next door in Hove for excitement. I was all set on going out to find a bit of adventure.

However, on my father's advice, I half-heartedly wrote to the Guernsey Growers' Association and they sent me four names of growers who might be interested in giving me employment. Even more half-heartedly, I twiddled a pin and wrote to a grower who turned out to be one of the most remarkable men I have ever met. I would not have missed my years in Guernsey for twenty million pounds. I was forced to admit that fathers sometimes know best!

I went over to Guernsey one bleak January morning in 1938 in the mail boat to have an interview with Raymond Ogier Falla. To my silent horror, my mother announced that she was coming with me. I more or less waved goodbye to any possibility of landing a job. What man in his senses would employ a girl who brought her mother to the interview? As I was not a bit keen, I really did not care what happened. But that was before we met R.O.F. as he was affectionately known throughout the island.

He had a dynamic personality. He was full of energy, enthusiasm and vigour. He was tall and dark, thin and shabby, driving a terrible rattling old car. He was married with three young children and a lovely old farm house. He was the biggest bulb and flower grower on the island. I had twiddled my pin magnificently, or may be the good fairies had guided my hand.

He whirled me into the job. He hustled a lady, who did not want me, into offering me lodgings. He said he would send for me in February when the daffodil season began. Neither my mother or I quite knew what had hit us. My mother fell for him hook line and sinker, so it was a case of "Guernsey, here I come!"

After my first day's work I decided that no power on earth would make me stay in the job. I did not know what I was doing to start with. I was in charge of a rough, tough-looking bunch of characters who deeply resented my presence. These were the women who bunched the flowers in dozens ready to be packed into boxes for market. It was snowing, a rare phenomenon in the Channel Isles.

We could have no heating in the flower sheds because of the precious flowers, so we had to suffer the draughts and icy chill. I had a rotten cold, and the chain came off my bike when I set off for my digs in the evening.

I ached in every limb being unaccustomed to standing all day. I started at 7.00 a.m. and finished at 6.00 p.m. and never have I known a longer or nastier day. My disillusionment was total.

When at last I struggled back to my digs, there was an enormous coal fire burning, the like of which I had never seen before, nor have I since. My landlord, bless him, was a coal merchant. My landlady was a superb cook and once I was warm and fed I began to take a less jaundiced view of my present mode of life.

"Maybe," I said to myself, "I won't catch tomorrow morning's boat back home. Maybe I'll give it a day or two. It can't be worse than today."

I am so thankful I did not go rushing back home. The three springs and two summers I worked in Guernsey turned out to be some of the happiest and most carefree days of my life.

My original arrangement with R.O.F. was that I should go for a three months' trial period. By mutual agreement, it was decided that I should stay on for the summer, I sent for my little £10 Morris which was a big improvement to my bike as my digs were three miles from the flower farm.

As the daffodils came flowing in, in greater and ever greater quantities, so the staff grew bigger and our hours progressively lengthened.

At the peak of the season, when we were sending six hundred boxes a day, we worked in the bunching sheds from 7.00 a.m. to 10.00 p.m., weekends as well. The bunching ladies went home then, and I joined the team of men actually packing the flowers into the boxes which was the nicest job of all. I used to go home at midnight, leaving the men to tie up, label and load the boxes on to the lorries to go down to catch the morning boat next day. The bulk went to Covent Garden but we sent boxes to markets all over the country.

The girls bunching the flowers were paid piece work. As I recall, the rate was about twopence a dozen bunches. They had been happily cheating R.O.F. for years. One of my jobs was to check their counts, hence my unpopularity. But we all eventually overcame our prejudices, and worked pretty well together. I was careful to be scrupulously fair, and never asked anyone to do anything that I was not prepared to do myself.

After working this strenuous day in the flower sheds I used to go back to my digs and start playing bridge. I never seemed to be tired. I loved every minute.

I used to career about with reckless abandon in my little car, often with my landlady's children. I remember the little boy, Dick, entered a fancy dress competition and had no idea about a suitable costume. As I had recently completed the St. John Ambulance first aid course, I suggested I should bandage him and he could call himself a casualty.

We went to work with a will with red ink for blood and I tied that poor child up so that he could scarcely move. As I assisted him to struggle out of the car, I overheard a bystander say, "There you are! I *knew* she'd knock someone down sooner or later!" It quite made my day!

From field to tying house, 1939.

Field of dancing daffodils; Guernsey, 19

R.O.F. grew several varieties of daffodils and these were followed in due season by tulips, iris and gladioli. We had great rushes of work with slack spells in between, when I used to take the opportunity to go home for a few days, or travel over to England. One year I crossed that stretch of Channel fourteen times. On the thirteenth trip, I was going back to Guernsey from England on the 13th of September, sleeping overnight in berth number thirteen. We were twenty-three hours late in fog. When I told the purser about this he said, "We always throw Jonahs overboard!" I never spent a more boring day. There was nothing to do but eat and I could not even do much of that as money was running out.

I made friends with a couple who came from the Midlands as my mother did. Pip was R.O.F.'s right hand and came from Stratford on Avon. His wife, Joan, came from Evesham. They had been married about six months. After more than forty years we are still great friends, and now live about twenty miles apart. This is another lifelong friendship that I cherish.

When war broke out in 1939, R.O.F. began to turn over some of his land to food production. Several of his men had joined up. Though I had enlisted in the Land Army, they had not sent for me, so I thought I would stay on in Guernsey until they did.

About six o'clock one morning in June, my mother telephoned me to say she thought I ought to come home. Dunkirk had happened, and like everyone else in Britain, I had been alternately incredulous, appalled and finally inspired by Churchill's rallying call to "blood, toil, tears and sweat." But champion ostrich that I was, it never occurred to me that all these shattering events in Europe would make any personal impact on me.

So when my mother phoned suddenly out of the blue, I thought at once of my father, whose health was a constant worry to mother. I felt he must be ill again and I had an arrangement with her that I would go home at once if she needed me. I did not ask her what the trouble was, but just said, "Do you want me for just a few days or shall I bring all my things?" She replied that I had better bring everything. This seemed to me to confirm my fears for my father.

I threw all my things into my trunk which then would not shut. My landlord kindly cut down their clothes-line and roped it together with that. I raced away to explain my sudden departure to R.O.F. and say "Au revoir". I had every expectation of returning sooner or later. I never did.

I can see R.O.F. now, in my mind's eye, leaning out of an upstairs window of his house and saying, "I don't think it's your father, Margaret. The future of these islands is crumbling to dust. Your mother is right to have you home."

I made less than nothing of all this, and when I saw mother standing alone on the pier to meet me, I was more sure than ever that something was wrong with father.

Thankfully, in one way, my forebodings were quite incorrect, and my father was fine. My mother had been asked to open and equip an A.R.P. hospital and needed my help. Nobody, until after Dunkirk, had imagined we should need such a place. So mother and I and a band of nurses and other volunteers threw ourselves into this enterprise and worked like furies for about forty-eight hours.

Then came the heart-stopping announcement that we were going to be an "undefended open town" and would most likely be occupied by the Germans.

It was very difficult to believe it. Imagination fairly boggled. As in 1914, we told each other that the war could not last long and it would "be all over by Christmas."

I wonder how we would have felt had we known then that the German occupation would last for five years all but a month?

CHAPTER THREE

My War 1940-1945

I do not suppose it is medically possible for a human heart to stop beating, then pick up again of its own volition. I can only say that is what I felt my heart did, the first time I saw a German plane flying at roof-top level over the island.

I had half-pretended to myself that perhaps the Germans would not bother themselves with such little unimportant places. We had no fortifications or industries that they could use. Jersey is the biggest of the group and that measured twelve miles by eight. However, the German High Command thought otherwise. I was told that they were very proud to be treading on British soil.

We had about a week from the day we were declared an open town, until the Germans actually arrived.

About half the population evacuated, something like 30,000. Most of the young men went, on official advice.

My parents, on three separate occasions, suggested it would be a good idea if I went to England. My sister was already there nursing with Queen Alexandra's Nursing Service.

I must say I was not much help. Each time they tackled me on the subject, I shouted that I would *not* go without them and rushed out of the house in floods of tears. There was never any question of my father leaving the bank, and it would have taken more than a German army to prise my mother from his side, so really, we had no choice. Once we agreed upon this, we settled down to await the worst.

There were many tragic scenes on the pier when families were parted, many mothers and children going to England with what they could carry, leaving husbands and fathers behind.

Evacuees were allowed to take £20 each with them. Many who left had never been away from the Island before, and had no friends or relatives on the mainland to contact.

My father paid me the biggest compliment I think I have ever had. He asked me to go with him to the bank.

"I want you to help me steady the staff," he said. I do not suppose for a moment I was a help to anyone, but it helped me to live through the days of waiting.

There were immense queues of people waiting to draw their pitiful £20. I do not remember any hysteria but an awful lot of people fainted because of the long wait in the sunny June weather.

Ever since I was a little girl I had heard my father speak of "the strong room". This had fascinated me but I was never allowed to see it. I thought to myself, "Now's my chance to see this mysterious place. I'll ask someone to take me down when they are not so busy."

It is a very strange thing, because *I know* I was taken to the strong room, but I cannot remember a single detail about it. I suppose the strange and abnormal pressures we were undergoing were so great, that my mind was simply numb.

A very great number of pets were destroyed that week. People who were leaving obviously could not take their pets with them, and those of us who were staying felt it would not be right to keep animals who would need feeding. Our cats were so spoilt, having liver every week, and cuts off the joint, we could not have borne to see them hungry.

The animal's shelter had a terrible time, putting down literally thousands of beautiful dogs and cats. I must say we were very upset, but everything was so awful we seemed to be doing things in cold blood that one would not have thought possible. The whole thing was an unbelievable nightmare.

We had a very good Bretonne maid who had been with us for some time and we were all very fond of her. I do not know who first thought of it, but it was decided that Marie should come down from the top floor and sleep with me. I think we had some confused idea that if we were going to be raped, murdered or merely beaten up or bombed, it would be a comfort if we were all together.

Marie and I started to bring her bed down from the floor above. My mother, from sheer force of habit, stood at the foot of the stairs, calling; "Mind the walls, girls, mind the walls!" I laughed so much I nearly dropped my end of the bed, but nobody else seemed to think it was funny. When one thinks how the bottom had dropped violently out of our world and we were awaiting heaven alone knew what horrors, it was incredible how my mother clung to some semblance of normality.

Marie heard about General de Gaulle and wanted to join him in England. She had a fierce hatred of "Le Boche". Her brother and fiancé and numerous cousins were in the French army.

When my father came home that day I said to him, "Marie wants to go. She's heard about the Free French. She's packing now."

My father had borne a number of appalling blows in the last few days and was worn out.

"That's just about the worst news yet," he said. Marie overheard him and, bursting into tears, vowed she would stay with us. It was as well for her she did, as Ives, her fiancé, managed to escape from France, and they eventually married. In the meantime she was a tremendous source of help and strength to us all.

My father was very worried about the considerable sum of money in bearer bonds and gold bullion held by the bank. He kept ringing head office in London who only said there was some difficulty with the insurance and would my father please hold on for a few more days. But time was running out and my father was determined to get that money away. He took the matter into his own hands. Before the war there were only the big five banks in the Channel Islands. Today there are dozens of merchant banks. The five managers met and decided to join forces and stop the Germans laying a finger on their gold and bonds.

My father sent for a lorry and a number of old potato sacks. Several million pounds worth of bullion and bonds were bundled into the sacks and whisked off, accompanied by two of my father's clerks. I heard afterwards that their troubles only began when they reached Weymouth. Nobody would believe them and they had the greatest difficulty persuading anyone to help them. One man sat on the pile of sacks on the quay, whilst the other struggled with authority from a public phone box.

The Germans were not particularly pleased to find the strong rooms empty, but no one was victimised. For which mercy we were very thankful.

I heard that my one-time employers, the lady-gardener partnership, had evacuated, so I swiftly set about obtaining one of their abandoned gardens for our own use.

I was very lucky indeed in being able to take over a lovely walled fruit garden, very near where we lived. There was plenty of space for vegetable growing and that summer I began to save my own seed. I am quite sure this garden saved my sanity and moreover, helped us survive as we were virtually vegetarians for the following five years.

A plane dropped messages ordering us to paint white flags in the Royal Square in the centre of St. Helier, and at the airport. Every house had to fly a white flag. There was a lengthy list of what we had to do, or not to do. Punishment for disobedience was deportation or death. I shall never forget the sight of those white flags hanging from every house. It was both sickening and demoralising, and I never felt more depressed in my life.

Before the Germans actually dropped their orders, but after we had been declared an open town, we had a tiny taste of war at close quarters. I think the Germans wanted to test the truth of the statement that we really were unfortified. They sent a wave of planes over, machine-gunning all over the island, killing and injuring people on the beach, in the fields and in the town. In Guernsey it was much worse because the mailboat was in harbour and it carried a gun.

It would have been better if the gun crew had not opened fire on the German planes because the aircraft retaliated by sweeping the whole pier with machine-gun bullets. There were queues of people waiting to board the boat and the whole area was reduced to a shambles. Even the ambulance was riddled with bullets.

We were totally unprepared for anything like this, and I think it was the following day that our ordeal of waiting was over and our ordeal of occupation began.

My practical mother put large safety pins in all my jackets and coats and I was instructed to "mark" any soldier who attacked me! I did not enquire how I was to do this because I could see she was happier thinking I was armed with a pin! Marie gave me some useful tips in the art of self preservation. Actually, I have to say that the German rank and file behaved very correctly at all times so far as I know. By and large, if one managed to keep out of their way, one stayed out of trouble. One could expect no mercy if caught disobeying their orders.

I can almost count on the fingers of one hand the times I was forced to address any member of the occupying force.

They came to search our house on three separate occasions, on one pretext or another. I remember there was a frightful battering on the front door one night after we had all gone to bed. My mother and I opened the door and in rushed three Germans, one officer and two men with their bayonets fixed.

"What do you want?" we asked.

"We are looking for a man. You have a man in this house?" the officer replied.

"Yes there is a man here. It is my father and he is ill in bed. Please don't let your men rush in on him," I said.

He motioned the men to wait and went into look at my father himself for which kindness I do not suppose I was really grateful enough at the time. They then went on to look for their "man" in all the drawers!

They changed the rule of the road so we had to ride our bikes on the right hand side, whilst they flashed by in *our* cars. I inadvertently broke this traffic rule one day and two military police made me get off my bike.

"You pay fine, five marks," they told me.

"I don't understand," I tried, "I don't speak German." Though their English was quite good.

We kept this up for a bit then they lost patience and laid hold of my bike. "If you won't pay fine, we take bike," they told me.

I climbed down in a hurry and paid them their beastly five marks which amounted to about 10s/6d. I would have been in a terrible plight without my cycle.

Another time I had direct contact with the Germans was when they came to fetch our car. We had registered her as older than she was, in the hope of saving her, because they were taking the newer cars first. Though my parents had never driven very much because they had taken it up rather late in life, we still did not want our Wolsley to fall into enemy hands. However, they took her in the end.

They paid our officials in marks for all these cars but we were not reimbursed until after the war was over.

At the very beginning of the occupation, the army was very anxious to make friends with the civilians. I was accosted one day by two very grand looking officers, when I was in Boots the Chemists. I fled upstairs and ran into a friend who enquired with astonishment, "What on earth's wrong, Margaret? You look all hot and bothered."

"They *spoke* to me," I gasped, half furious and half frightened. We had been warned not to antagonise them, and I had no idea what the Germans considered was antagonism.

As long as the news was good for the Germans, we were allowed to keep our radios. But when we started to win the Battle of Britain in the air, they were quickly called in.

Some very brave people kept their sets, discovery for disobeying this order was punished by deportation.

I heard of a quick-witted young mother who caught sight of a German search party approaching her house. She whipped the radio into the baby's pram, dumped the child on top and met the Germans on her doorstep.

"Certainly you can search the house," she told them. "I always take my baby out at this time of day, and I don't want to alter her routine. You carry on. I won't be long." And she sailed out in safety.

Other people were not so lucky, many were deported and some were never heard of again.

Several people I knew very well gave me reason to believe that they were listening to the news, but we had an elaborate pretence that they had heard it from someone else and were just passing it on. One could not be too careful. It took me years after the war to break myself of the habit of glancing over my shoulder before I spoke.

All my friends in my immediate neighbourhood could tell if the news was good or bad by the way I cycled back from my daily visit to the town, where I garnered what news I could.

If I cycled by like mad with my legs going like pistons they knew that either there was a batch of Red Cross letters in, or I had heard some heartening news. If I pedalled by slowly and dejectedly they knew that whatever I had managed to hear was depressing.

It was ten months before we received a message from England through the Red Cross. It consisted of twenty-five words and was six months old. We had had the same postman for years. He was a V.C. from the first world war and was a real friend of the family. The first message came from my sister who had a really very tough war, not knowing how we were faring. Poor Postman Counter was so thrilled to bring us a message, and was quite shattered when I burst into tears before I even opened it. It was wonderful to get a message but they were so brief and frustrating. We were so longing to hear some real news of all our relatives and friends in England. My father used to say, "I don't understand you. You curse when you receive a message and you curse when you don't." It was not strictly true but very nearly so.

And talking of cursing, I was a sad trial to my father who could not bear to hear a woman swear, and I really could not help it, every time I thought of the Germans. I only ever said a mild "damn and blast" in front of him, but he thought this was terrible.

"I can't think where you ever learned such awful language," he would complain, more in sorrow than in anger. If he had only known it, I had picked up some splendid swear words in both French and English in the flower sheds in Guernsey. Happily, I managed never to let him hear them. I practised them on Marie, however, and she used to make me laugh by turning quite pale, and crossing herself. I had no idea what it all meant, but Marie's reaction was very gratifying.

I never dreamed that there would be any fraternisation or collaboration with the occupying forces but once more I was wrong.

Girls, I suppose, in any country, will be girls. With hindsight, I am truly grateful to the girls who were willing to oblige the Germans. It did make the place a lot safer for those of us who could not bear the sight of them.

French prostitutes were brought over and were installed in one of the hotels. Our Jersey doctors were forced to examine these girls regularly as V.D. seemed to be a real bogey in the German army. Other armies, too, I daresay.

The Governor, who represented the Crown in the Channel Islands, was a military man, and had naturally left with all the other military personnel. The full responsibility for the welfare of the civilian population fell on the shoulders of the Bailiff. Poor man, there was just no precedent for him to follow.

Mr. Coutanche, who later became Sir Alexander Coutanche, was a legal man, and he called to mind a document called the Geneva Convention. This, apparently, set down the duties of an occupying power, and Mr. Coutanche quoted from this *ad nauseum*. The German commanders came and went over the years. Some, I believe, were easier to deal with than others. Mr. Coutanche came in for a lot of criticism but I believe he did his best in an impossible situation.

To begin with there was a good supply of food in the shops, which of course lasted no time at all. My Guernsey employer, Raymond Falla, was the first person to take any positive steps towards the problem of feeding us.

As a start, on his own land, he ploughed in all his bulbs a foot deep and started growing crops on top of them. Five years later, he ploughed the bulbs up again, and amazingly, he had a nucleus of stock to restart his flower farm.

He persuaded the Germans, and our own authorities to allow him to travel to France to see what he could do by way of starting up some kind of business deal with the French. We needed grain, both for seed and milling, vegetable seeds and indeed practically any staple food in bulk.

This was a brave man and a far-seeing one. I have always maintained he was the national hero of the Channel Isles. Without his efforts I am sure we would have starved. The occupying forces, according to the Geneva Convention, were supposed to feed us. The fact was, we seemed to be feeding them.

Raymond Falla had to travel on a German barge which stood a very good chance of being attacked by the R.A.F. If he survived the sea trip, the Germans were quite likely to have him arrested as a British spy. Furthermore, the French were in no mood, at that time, to assist anyone who professed to be British. Anyway, they needed all the food there was for themselves. He once told me he half-expected to feel a knife in his back at any time.

How he persuaded the French to do business with him I shall never know. He spoke the language fluently and colloquially. Perhaps that helped. Perhaps it was his personal charm and magnetism or maybe his complete integrity. He went about France with suitcases of German marks, and carried his tooth-brush and shaving-brush in his coat pocket.

On his first mission he went alone. No one else, in either island, seemed willing to run the risks he was taking. When he came back, not only alive, but successful, he was able to enlist others to accompany him on future trips.

R.O.F.'s wife and children had been evacuated. The Guernsey evacuation had been organised differently from ours. All the children went *en bloc* with their schools. I heard afterwards of a family of five all being sent on different boats. Most of these were cargo boats, sometimes coal boats, so the plight of the evacuees was pretty ghastly.

R.O.F. managed to set up a steady, if small, trickle of essentials such as flour, salt, butter, macaroni, cheese, meat and sugar. We never had all these luxuries in the same week, of course. Mostly, a week's ration of meat for four people came home in my coat pocket. Camembert cheese seemed to be the only cheese available which always arrived more than overripe. The smell was very off-putting. I have never been able to face camembert since.

When salt became unobtainable, I used to go down to the beach with bottles and bring back sea water. There were gaps in the defences which I could squeeze through. Mined areas were clearly marked with skull and cross-bones and the words, "Achtung! Minen!"

The sea water gave an ounce and a half of sparkling salt from a pint-and-a-half bottle when it was evaporated down. If one did not want to go to that trouble, one could boil the vegetables in the sea water just as it was.

To supplement the flour ration, I would go gleaning in the fields after the harvest. We ground the grain in a coffee mill and the result was a very good coarse porridge.

Potatoes, if you had enough of them to spare, could be made into potato flour which was a splendid substitute for corn flour. It took a lot of time and trouble but was worth it.

A loaf of bread was in colour, shape and size like a brick. It was made from sour dough and mixed with sea water. Everything was rationed and there was never enough of anything.

We thought that at least we would have plenty of fish but we could not have been more wrong. The Germans commandeered 80% of the catch as a start. They sent an armed guard out with each fishing boat with instructions to cut the nets and bring the boats back at the slightest sign of aerial or naval activity. As the nets were irreplacable, naturally the fishermen resented all this, and very few of them went out. Who could blame them?

We had limpets and razor-fish and spider-crabs that could be collected from the shore. I remember having a hearty laugh in a grocer's one day. The enterprising man had collected and cooked and chopped up some limpets, and had then mixed them with cold mashed potatoes. We were not fussy, but this looked revolting. He offered some of his "fish cakes" to a lady customer in front of me, who gave them one shuddering glance and said, "Don't tempt me!"

Sugar beet treacle was a good wholesome substitute. If you cooked it long enough it became very thick and black and was quite palatable. We had to grate the beet, boil it, strain it and then boil again. It took hours and our houses were permeated with the smell. We wore out all our graters and made new ones by banging a few nail holes into a tin lid.

Tea and coffee were made from pretty well anything. The residue from the sugar-beet was quite good, dried off and browned in the oven. Some people favoured carrot or parsnip tea or coffee, grated and dried and/or mixed with dried apple peelings or dried pea shucks. I found some little lupin seeds were very good when toasted and ground in the coffee-mill and mixed with home-grown grated chicory. The thing they all had in common was they were all brown and wet.

It seems unbelievable today, but before the war all the trades' people delivered one's shopping. The grocer even called for his order, and the bread, meat and fish, etc, were all sent round to the house. We had our tea delivered from a specialist shop and when the man brought round the last ration he handed it over and said, "This is the last of the tea, Mrs Vaudin. What ever will you do?"

My mother drew herself up to her full height and cast him a withering glance. "Do?" she repeated. "Do? We'll do without, of course." We tended to adopt this remark as our personal slogan.

Fuel became a problem. Towards the latter half of the occupation, the gas was turned off at the main most of the time. We were allowed half-an-hour to cook breakfast, one hour at middle day and another half-an-hour in the evening. We made great use of a haybox which kept things hot and even continued to cook such items as beetroot or vegetable stew, on the same principle, I suppose, as the slow cooker does today.

I had a little cart I called "Aid'er". This was a tea-chest on pram wheels, in which I used to carry all sorts of things including buckets of tar from the gasworks. We then mixed this with leaves or twigs or sawdust and spooned the mixture on to the sitting-room fire. It made a fine blaze but I cannot describe the mess.

In the early days, the Germans decided to issue identity cards and had us all photographed. Rumour had it that the better-looking girls would be taken to Germany. The day I had to have my photograph taken, I neither washed my face or brushed my hair and I fixed my face in what I called my "German look". This was a sullen glare. The result was most gratifying. I might have been a survivor from an open boat after days at sea. Alternatively, I might have been mistaken for a prison guard from Belsen. (Though, of course, we knew nothing about those horror camps then.)

If they had started taking the better-looking girls away, I would have been the very last to go.

My friend, Marjorie, who was as sweet-natured as she was beautiful, and could not have made herself look disagreeable under any circumstances, had a very difficult time. Germans were for ever following her. She took to dodging into shops and leaving by the back entrance when she was having trouble in the town. Thankfully, nothing terrible happened to her but it was a continual anxiety. I had known Majorie since dancing-school days, when we were about six years old. We were good friends at school and I do not know what I should have done without her companionship during the dark days.

Everything was in short supply or non-existent. I used to clean my teeth with soot which was disgusting but effective. The shortage of tobacco and cigarettes struck cruelly at the habitual smokers but we got over this problem by growing and curing our own.

Soap was one thing for which we did not seem to be able to find a substitute. I remember once telling one of my friends, "The sheets look grey, hanging on the line. I thought the sun might bleach them. And the towels are worse."

She comforted me with these words, "Never mind, dear. They've been passed through the water and pegged out in the air."

As for toilet soap we were very well placed. My mother had attended numerous bazaars and coffee mornings for years. And she *always* bought soap. This was grand as we could help out those of our friends who were *in extremis*, besides staying moderately clean ourselves.

In 1940, the merchants who exported tomatoes in the summer had already stocked up with the coloured tissue-paper with which they lined the trays and boxes. This paper found its way into the retail seed shops and we were thankful to be able to buy it, cut it into squares and use it for toilet paper. I was quite overcome with giggles one day when kind Mrs. Jeune, at the seed shop I favoured, pressed some white tissue paper into my shopping bag, murmuring, "I'm sure Mr. Vaudin would prefer white." As it happened my father was colour-blind!

The same lady wiped the smile off my face on another day when I went in to buy some lime for my garden.

"I'm sorry," she said, "We have got some lime but we aren't allowed to sell it."

"Why not?" I asked quite exasperated. "Who says you can't?"

She kept shaking her head and muttering under her breath. At last she came out with the reason in a whisper, "We aren't supposed to mention it, Miss Vaudin. But if we should have an epidemic, lime is the only thing we have to cover the bodies . . ."

My blood ran cold. By this time there were hundreds of displaced persons living under appalling conditions and an epidemic of cholera was by no means an impossibility.

My sister and I, 1927.

These displaced persons were the most tragic and desparate people I have ever seen. They came from all over the Continent and Africa too.

They had been brought over to the islands to build fortifications to complete Hitler's Atlantic Wall. They also built underground munition dumps and hospitals. The Germans never meant to send them home again, where ever home was. The poor souls worked, and died where they worked. Those that survived were taken, I have been told, to extermination camps in Alderney.

I had a lot of trouble at one time with the drivers of the German vehicles that parked outside my garden. The house opposite belonged to our old doctor, as did my garden. I rented it from his widow, a frail old lady who had moved away to live with her daughter. Her home had been requisitioned by the Organisation Todt, the branch of the German army in charge of the displaced persons. The guards wore khaki, and the first time I saw a man in this uniform I thought a miracle happened and we had been relieved overnight. I started to run, then hastily stopped when he turned and I saw the swastika on his armband. It was a cruel blow!

The Todt drivers used to park their lorries and cars right on the pavement, close to my only entrance and exit, so that I could not get in or out with my bike, barrow or "Aid'er". Many a time I stormed into poor Dr. Hind's old home calling out, "Does anyone here speak English?"

Nine times out of ten I was greeted with titters of laughter as a number of local people worked there. The Germans gave extra rations to the Jersey people they employed. One could not blame them, I suppose, but I did not look upon them with a favourable eye in those days. I could have hit them but they used to get the trucks moved for me.

I was afraid the Germans might force me to sell my produce to them, or worse, they might even take it. But the garden was too small for them to bother with, though it was plenty big enough to grow a lot of food for my family and friends. Behind the high stone walls I found an oasis of peace and tranquillity.

When I took over the garden there was a crop of cabbage ready for cutting. Imagine my delight when I cleared this away to discover the cabbage had been intercropped with young strawberry plants. I picked one hundredweight of strawberries every year. This without nets or straw. How popular I was in the strawberry season! All our particular friends and the very old or very young were on my list of customers. Never, before or since, have I seen such beautiful big cherries, both white and black. Apples, pears and figs were all superb too. It is with a pang when I last passed my garden when visiting Jersey to see that it was a concrete waste, having been turned into an ambulance station.

It was very strange, but we ran short of stamps. We had no occasion to write to anyone, but nevertheless we had no penny stamps. We bisected United Kingdom 2d. stamps, thus making two one-penny stamps. These have now become collectors' items. After a while both islands issued their own stamps which has proved a very lucrative business in the post-war years.

Another thing that used to rouse me to fury was to hear the Germans singing. When marching through the town, the troops would often be ordered to sing. An N.C.O. would shout a command, followed by a count, "Eine, zwei, drei," and they would start to sing which maddened me.

"We have nothing to sing about," I said to myself, "So why should we have to listen to them?"

"I wish they'd *choke*!" I used to say with some violence. I had no tolerance at all and kicked against the pricks all the time.

My father, though he held the opinion that everyone in the world had their good points, and every country had a right to have a point of view, and various other Christian and infuriating doctrines, he drew the line at shaking hands with the Germans. They called on him frequently at the bank and they just loved to click their heels and shake hands with civilians. My father told me he always had pens and papers and files in *both* hands whenever they appeared.

Miss Fraser, the lady who used to teach cookery in the States Cookery School before the war, had her premises converted to a soup kitchen. She had a band of voluntary helpers and amused me very much one day by showing me a particularly revolting smelly dishcloth. She kept this handy and brandished this about in her right hand whenever the Germans chose to inspect her kitchen. It sounds childish but it made us laugh.

The worst thing that happened began on a lovely September in 1942. Out of the blue, there was a notice in the German-controlled local paper.

"All English-born men, between the ages of seventeen and seventy together with their wives and children, to be deported to Germany immediately."

My father, being a Jerseyman, born and bred, was not directly affected. But our poor friends . . . We had so many English-born friends. Where would it all end? I began to worry about my mother who was English-born. When the opportunity occurred I asked the Bailiff if he could arrange to substitute my name for hers if her name ever appeared on a deportation list.

We heard that this measure of wholesale deportation by the Germans was taken as some kind of reprisal for something of which we had never heard. It was quite the most heart-breaking period we had to endure.

Our friends kept coming to see us that first day to say "goodbye". They brought us their wills and their gold watches and jewellery or whatever possessions they held most dear, with the requests that we would see that their relations in England received them one day. Strong men broke down and wept. I had never seen a man cry before, and it unnerved me.

There were extraordinary scenes at the Deanery, the Dean being head of the Church of England in the absence of the Bishop of Winchester, to whose diocese the island was attached.

The Dean married six couples at a time. Girls with English fathers married their Jersey boy-friends in order to stay in the island. Jersey girls married their English-born boy-friends so that they could go with them.

That first day we were worried about a particular couple, a Mr. and Mrs. Tice, both born in England. They were in their sixties and not in very good health. Mr. Tice was our dentist. They were living in an area several miles from town which had been taken over almost entirely by the Germans. There were no phones by then and the Tices had no relatives in the Island.

My mother kept saying to me, "You must go out to see the Tices."

I would start getting my bike out then I would hear her calling me again: "Don't go for a minute. I can see someone else coming down the path."

So back I went again and this went on till curfew, and then I dared not go. We worried about them all night.

"I'll go the minute curfew lifts in the morning. I wish we could have got a message to them *somehow*!" I said.

Morning brought the news that Mr. and Mrs. Tice had decided not to go to Germany. Mrs. Tice was dead and Mr. Tice deeply unconscious. They had stretched themselves out beside the gas cooker.

Mr. Tice must have wanted to see his wife safely away, and before his end came the gas must have been turned off from the main and he was found too soon. He was taken to the Nerve Hospital and kept there for the rest of the war.

From that day to this I have been unable to put off anything until tomorrow. No matter how trivial it is, *I have to do it now.*

It seemed so dreadful to me that they were so alone and never knew how much we were thinking of them and suffering with them. Theirs was not an isolated incident. There were quite a few people who preferred death to deportation.

During these sad days, someone—I never knew whom—inserted a few words in the local paper each evening; it was printed in heavy black type and I can quote it still:

> "Tread gaily,
> Yet not unaware,
> His feet have counted every stair,
> Thy feet must climb."

Apart from the shock and despair of this deportation, we were justly furious at the Germans differentiating between us. We were all British and we were deeply resentful at being treated differently, one from another.

My father's health by this time was at a very low ebb, but he made a very gallant and successful effort to save some of his staff from being deported.

Five of the staff were involved. Three of them were married, and two of them had delicate children.

My father got on his bike and struggled up the hill to the German H.Q. He swore he could not keep his branch open without the help of his three key men. This was, of course, quite untrue, as there was so little business to do, I should think it could have functioned perfectly with one man and a boy.

Amazingly, the Germans agreed with him, and undertook to remove the names of the three married men from the list.

At a tense and emotional staff meeting, my father announced that the married men with families were safe. He had to tell the younger men that he dared not push his luck any further, and he was so very sorry he could not tell them they too were safe.

I am happy to be able to say that both the men survived the ordeal and came home at the end of the war.

In the meantime, what local Red Cross volunteers we had in the Island quickly mobilised themselves for action. They collected a few comforts and insisted on being present on the pier to see the deportees away on the boats that were to take them to France en route for German prison camps.

These boats were really shocking. There was nowhere to sit under cover. They were little holiday river boats. The only drinking water was on deck in a few milk churns.

Sister Lister, who was a Royal Red Cross Nurse, a survivor from a sunken hospital ship in the Dardanelles, asked me to help.

"Sister," I said, "Please don't ask me. I really could not bear it. I cannot and will not go."

She gave me one look and replied as if I had not spoken. "Here's your Red Cross armlet. I'll see you on the pier. The German pier patrol have been told to let us through."

I went. Never have I seen such courage. I remember carrying a little girl who was whimpering a little. Her mother turned on her fiercely, "Be quiet! Don't you *dare* let the Germans see you crying." The child stopped at once.

A young girl was wearing a skein of wool around her neck. I said to her, "That's a good idea."

She replied brightly, "Yes, isn't it? The wool will keep me warm on the journey and it will be something to do when we get there. I like knitting!"

When I was not carrying babies or suitcases, I mingled with the passengers already on the boat, sitting calmly on narrow wooden benches. I was shocked to see several of my parents' friends, all in their sixties, and none showing any visible signs of distress.

"You know," one lady said to me in a low voice, "You know, we'll never reach France. The Navy will intercept us, you see, and we'll be in England before you!"

"But of course you will," I replied, trying to hide my distress. "I'm sure you're right. You'll be in England in next to no time."

As it had all happened with such shattering speed, I could not see how they could possibly have heard about it in England but we kept up this cheerful pretence for hours. "Repatriation" was another word we bandied about. We said anything to send them off with a gleam of hope.

As the boats pulled away from the quay, they began to sing. I heard strains of *There'll always be an England* and *Old Lang's Syne*.

I could not stand any more and after a final wave I hurried away by myself, crying as though my heart had really broken. Through a mist of tears I saw a German officer step forward as if to speak to me. I gave him such a look of pure hatred that he moved back again. I have often wondered since what he would have said to me.

Would he have tried to say a word of reassurance? Was he going to taunt me? I shall never know, but I rather wish I had not looked at him so vindictively.

To this day, I cannot think about those scenes on the pier in September 1942, without tears coming to my eyes.

Thankfully I can report that thanks to the International Red Cross, the vast majority of those deportees lived to return to the Islands. But had the Red Cross not found them in time it would have been a very different story.

Where there is a shortage, inevitably there will be a black market. I overheard a dear innocent lady asking in a despairing voice, "But where *is* the black market? I can't find it anywhere!"

When everything was as bad as it could be for Britain, it was interesting that an English pound note could buy anything on the black market in France or Jersey, that would be denied to anyone offering German marks.

All the farm animals had to be registered with the Germans who kept checking to make sure the farmers were not killing beasts for their own consumption. The Germans, of course, commandeered for their own use, whatever they wanted, whenever they wanted it.

The farmers evolved a splendid scheme to circumvent this order An animal would mysteriously die, and the German would be summoned to inspect it. As soon as they had gone, the corpse would be rushed to another farm, where the farmer would again notify the Germans, who again came to inspect it. The second farmer, to keep the records straight, would be able to kill—let us say it was a pig—and share the meat with his friends and neighbours. The original dead pig would travel on, with any luck, to five or six other farms, in each case the farmer being able to kill another pig and everything would be more or less legal and tidy! For the loss of one pig, half a dozen could be slaughtered for civilian use. This amusing little ploy could not be perpetrated very often, obviously, but it did work now and again.

"Exchange and Mart" flourished. There was a fascinating column of advertisements in the local paper each evening. One might read:

"Baby rabbits in exchange for sugar." "Butter in exchange for tea." "One pound of sugar for what?" "One cake of soap in exchange for tobacco."

My three aunts came to Christmas Day dinner each year. I think we bartered soap most years but in 1944 my father came up with an idea that distressed us.

"I shall never play golf again, you know," he said to us one day. "Why don't you barter my golf shoes and tweed suit?"

We knew he was right but it seemed dreadful to barter his clothes. A friendly farmer was delighted with the exchange but mother and I were not very happy over this transaction.

Medicines and anaesthetics were perpetually in short supply. When my mother had an acute attack of gall-bladder pain, there were no anaesthetics available at that particular time. She looked terrible and I was convinced she was going to die. Miraculously, she recovered without surgery.

I was very lucky when I stuck a digging-fork through my toe. I was happily digging potatoes, wearing a pair of filthy old tennis shoes. My ground had been nicely manured with horse-droppings as I had a friend who was a road sweeper. (It was strange what a lot of horse-drawn vehicles the Germans used.) In horror, I stood on one foot and watched my tennis shoe turn from grey to red, then dashed for my bike to go and see the doctor.

"We haven't had any anti-tetanus vaccine for months," he told me. "I'll try the hospital, and see if the Germans will part with any."

I do not suppose I was properly grateful at the time, but the Germans did release a dose of anti-tetanus vaccine for me. I do not know what would have happened to me if they had not been so co-operative. Imagination tends to boggle, as I understand death from lockjaw is a terrible way to end one's life.

As the years passed our general health deteriorated somewhat. Minor ailments like boils and chilblains tended not to clear up. I started coughing and my mother was sure I was going T.B. I did not but lots of young people did.

I never left the house without telling my parents where I was going and what time I would be back. I only failed them once by being very overdue, and it certainly was not my fault.

Some friends of mine had a beautiful rose garden and for some reason known only to themselves, they liked me to undertake the spring pruning.

The garden was seven miles away from my home and by 1944 I really had not the energy to contemplate cycling all that way and doing a day's work as well. So for the first and last time I took the bus. It was run on charcoal and it made the one trip out and back from the town each day and again at night.

I was more than careful to check the exact time and place from which this bus departed. The outward journey was fine, and I was waiting contentedly enough at the bottom of the hill, where I had been told to wait. Imagine my feelings when I heard the bus turning at the *top* of the hill, leaving me to make my own way home. Dusk was falling and curfew was not all that far away.

There were no phones and no taxis. Any car from whom I might have hitched a lift would be driven by the Germans. I timed myself by my watch, five minutes running and five minutes walking. It seemed to take for ever.

My mother was waiting at the garden gate and asked a question and made a statement in the same breath, "The bus never came?" Satisfied that there was nothing amiss with me beyond exhaustion, she added, "You'd better go straight to bed and I'll bring you up a cup of cocoa."

I cheered up at once at this, as cocoa was a rare treat, not to say luxury. Like real tea which we only had on birthdays and Christmas and then went on boiling up the tea leaves over and over again.

I felt quite elated until I was attacked with cramp in both legs as soon as I got into bed. At that precise moment all the lights went off, and my mother gave a wail from the stairs, "Margaret, I daren't move in case I spill your cocoa. Have you got a match handy? Can you come and help me?"

"I've got cramp in both legs," I shrieked back, "I can't move either!" There was really only one thing to do, so we did it. We began to laugh!

My father's precarious health finally broke down in the autumn of 1942. His tremendous tussle with the Germans to save his staff was about the last straw. He had several fainting attacks and his breathing became very laboured and distressed. He more or less took to his bed in the winter months but recovered a little in the summer.

My mother was a great believer in "casting your bread on the waters." How right she was. If we shared our last crust (metaphorically speaking) with one friend, it was quite certain that another friend would turn up and share something with us.

With this in mind, I remember how my mother's charitable work repaid her a thousand times over.

When Roselle and I were both at school, she looked round for some public voluntary work. She was a wonderful organiser, and was invited to take over the district Nursing association. In those days the funds were raised entirely by voluntary contributions. There were only two nurses in St. Helier when she took over, and no nurses whatever in the country parishes. She sallied forth, arranging meetings and raising money until there were trained nurses working all over the Island.

When my father became almost bedridden, these nurses were so good to us. Towards the end of the war, when he seemed to be at death's door, they used to arrange to meet in couples at our house at least once and sometimes twice a day. It was so much more comfortable for a very sick person to be handled by trained nurses, especially when they were so very kind.

The last winter was the worst of all. In 1944, the allies invaded Normandy. D-Day was in June and we were perfectly certain we would be free long before the next winter. We could not believe our eyes when we saw that the Germans were making no effort to get back to the Continent. It took us some time to realise that—for our own sakes—we were being bypassed.

So we sat down to face another winter, this time with no gas or electricity and very little medical supplies.

The little Red Cross ship, the *Vega* saved us. To parody Mr. Churchill, "Never have so many, owed so much, to one little ship."

Once the allies landed in France, our trickle of food naturally dried up. Very soon the Germans were as hungry as we were. More so, I think, because we had had to tighten our belts gradually. They had had no experience of shortages so it hit them hard.

They started to eat our dogs and cats. I had a friend whose little Scottie went missing and then she found his head on her doorstep.

The *Vega* came in January 1945 for the first time. It was a terrible trip for a little ship. She had to go to a neutral port to be cleared. This port was Lisbon. And the same thing happened on the return trip. She had to cross the Bay of Biscay twice in mid-winter. The round trip took a month. A Swiss representative of the Red Cross travelled with her.

The *Vega* either brought us the most magnificent food parcels, we had one each, or she brought enough flour for us to have bread for a month. She could not bring both flour and parcels because of the lack of space.

The wonderful pure white flour produced a snow-white loaf which was a perfect picture and tasted delicious. The only thing that did not go quite right was that the entire Island became constipated. We were unused to such refined flour! I heard my mother suggesting people try boiled onions as there had been no laxatives in the shops for years.

I can remember every detail of the day we first received our parcels. I had fetched them in "Aid'er". I think they weighed about 10lbs in weight each. Some came from New Zealand and some from Canada.

There were tins of butter, marmalade, stew, corned beef and salmon. There was tea, dried milk and canned fruit.

My father was in bed and we plumped the parcels down beside him and it was like all the Christmases we had ever known rolled into one. It was all too good to be true. I think we were most thrilled with the tea.

In the middle of the excitement there was a knock on the front door. Thinking it would be a neighbour coming to rejoice over the food parcels, I danced to the door with my face all lit up with pleasure and anticipation Through a glass panel at the side of the door, I looked straight into the eyes of a German officer.

It nearly killed me. I only had one thought, "They've come for our parcels. They're going to take our parcels away from us. "I could not bear it.

Somehow I managed to open the door. He must have seen the appalling change in my expression because he said, "Please don't be frightened." He had come to search the house, again. What a shock he gave me! And I was mad with myself for letting him see I was upset.

To do the Germans justice, they never touched our parcels, hungry as they were. The Swiss Red Cross representative said this was because we had a "Pays Puissant" behind us. This warmed our hearts to think Britain was still GREAT Britain in German eyes.

About this time we decided that we had had about enough of living in a small island and thought we would like to live in England in the future. We thought perhaps if father could have some specialist treatment as soon as possible he might recover his health.

He decided to sell the house. Several people tried to persuade him not to burn his boats but to lease the house on a rent. He said he disapproved of absentee landlords and was determined to sell.

We actually sold our house in January 1945, giving possession on 1st June. We were so sure we would be liberated by then. We did, however, insert a prudent proviso in the contract, that if we were unable to go to England by June, we were to be allowed to stay on in the house with the use of the kitchen and bathroom plus two extra rooms of our choice.

Mercifully we did take this precaution, because, though we were liberated on 9th May, we were unable to leave the Island until the middle of June.

At the beginning of April my father fell suddenly even more ill than he had ever been before. Both the doctor and the nurses said he could not possibly recover.

We managed to arrange for a night nurse. It was very difficult for her, poor soul. The only light we could provide was a little aspirin bottle with a drop of paraffin in it. We made a hole in the lid and threaded a piece of string through which acted as a wick. If she wanted a hot drink in the night she had to light a fire in a minature incinerator we had concocted out of a paint tin.

After a couple of very distressing weeks, father showed marked signs of improvement, and to my consternation mother fell ill. I think it was partly exhaustion and strain, complicated by acute cystitis. She seemed very much inclined to turn her face to the wall.

This time the nurse came in by day to help me, whilst I slept in my parents' room to be on hand at night.

The war was so nearly over. I kept thinking how cruel it would be if both my parents died now after they had put up such a struggle.

People had been making crystal sets to hear the news when the power and batteries ran out. They fused lead and sulphur and cut off the telephone receiver to use as a headphone. It was on one of these contraptions we heard that the war in Europe was over.

At the same time we were faced with a new peril. The German commander in Jersey was a fanatic and did not want to surrender the Island. He decided to defend it to the last man.

They started digging slit trenches in our front gardens and road junctions. The German troops at this stage of the war were very young boys for the most part but this did not make us any happier and there were an awful lot of them.

Thankfully, the German commander in Guernsey was a sane man, and he overrulled his opposite number in Jersey. We heard on 9th May that we would be relieved that day. Winston Churchill referred to the

Col. Robinson; Liberator of Jersey. May 9th, 1945.

"dear Channel Islands" in the House of Commons. At last, we felt it really was all over.

The Germans confined themselves to barracks and we spent the morning scanning the sky for the R.A.F. and peering out to sea with binoculars to try and locate the Navy.

In the afternoon hundreds of us were crowded in the Royal Square waiting for something to happen. After a while I got restless and decided to walk down to the pier. On my way I met lots of others strolling aimlessly about. All of a sudden we became galvanised into action, and we all began to run, converging on one spot on the harbour wall. It was a most unforgettable moment. I was there when Colonel Robinson and ten men, took back the Islands for Great Britain. We tried to sing "God save the King", but we were all crying so much with joy, it was a poor effort.

Colonel Robinson climbed on to a bollard and told us he had seen the German commander and given him his orders. How we cheered! He had great difficulty in making his little speech as all the people nearest to him wanted to kiss him or shake his hand.

My old childhood friend Derek Dupre was among the relieving party. It was great seeing him again.

Medical supplies and food started pouring in and then came the letters. Our V.C. postman had remembered my sister's handwriting and handed her letter to my mother saying, "That's the one you're waiting for." He then dealt the rest out like a pack of cards. It was a wonderful day.

All the good news revived my parents in a most heart-warming way, and my father succeeded in surprising me again. "How are the German troops being taken away?" he asked me.

"Well," I explained as clearly as I could, "They load them into these amphibious lorries they call DUCKS. The troops are all in the country somewhere, you know. When they reach the beach, these lorries take to the water and go out to the troopships that are lying out in the bay."

My father thought about this for a bit and then said, "I wouldn't do it that way if I were in charge."

I asked him what he would do and my gentle and pacific father delivered his considered opinion,

"I'd make them march down from the country as a start," he said, "Then I'd march them to the end of the pier and I'd point to the troopships out in the bay, and I'd say, 'There's your Transport, now

swim'." I cannot tell you how much this amused and pleased me!

Our time in Jersey was running out. The people who had bought our house the previous January moved in. All our furniture went into storage, except what we were actually sitting on or sleeping in.

We lived in a decided muddle the last few weeks but we were quite accustomed to peculiar and uncomfortable conditions.

The King and Queen paid a visit to the islands almost before the last of the Germans had been removed. They certainly were given a tremendous and emotional welcome.

We were due to leave on the first passenger boat. It was a magical sight, dressed overall.

It was hard for my father to leave the island he had lived in all his life, and he loved Jersey very much.

I think he knew that he had not much longer to live, and he was anxious to see my mother settled near her own people. Her brother and two sisters had written welcoming letters.

So one sunny day in June 1945, with my father on a stretcher, we left Jersey and set off on our great removal.

Footnote

In 1980 Independent Television put on a serial play based on the Occupation of Guernsey. It was called *Enemy at the Door* and the theme music was poignantly haunting. Someone had set words to the tune: *Song of Freedom*

When you meet with fear and dangers
When the storms of winter blow
Look for mercy not in strangers
For your hope is nearer than you know.

Every blessing is within your reach
For you, alone, must shape your destiny
Be bold, and break the chains that bind you
And you'll find the kingdom of the free.

When there is no light to guide you
And the dark clouds hide the skies
Turn, my friend, and look inside you,
To the place where true salvation lies.

Raymond Falla, the last surviving member of the emergency committee in Guernsey was appointed technical advisor for *Enemy at the Door*. No longer young, he still retains his vitality of mind and body. He still has a twinkle in his eye and still shows his overwhelming interest in, and love for his island home. He was a legend in his own time.

Opposite: *Eagerness to change German Reich Marks back to "Real" (English) Money! Queues outside all the banks. May 1945; Jersey.*

CHAPTER FOUR

The Great Removal 1945-1954

I shall never forget seeing the coast of England rising out of the dawn mist that summer morning when we arrived from Jersey after the war was over.

The sea trip had taken us over fifteen hours because, we were told we had to thread our way through the minefields. Normally it takes nine hours. The boat, I remember, had been stripped of everything but the barest essentials. There were no doors, for instance, just a curtain hanging over the cabin entrance. There were ropes and rope ladders strung about around the staircase. The boat had obviously seen war service.

At 6.00 a.m. I was anxiously scanning the pier to see if the ambulance had arrived to carry father on the next leg of our journey.

I have always admired the work done by St. Johns Ambulance. I have had an even stronger affection for the brigade since that day when the two St. Johns men, Mr. Speke and Mr. Norgrove, took charge of us at Southampton and delivered us safely to Kidderminster. Years later Mr. Norgrove wrote about his work with the St. Johns Ambulance, and in his published article he mentioned that fetching the Vaudin family from Southampton after the war was one his most interesting assignments. I can add that on that day a mutual admiration society was born!

My relations, bless them, had also arranged for an estate van to meet us. This was an amazing piece of organisation on their part, as petrol was severely rationed in 1945, and only essential journeys were authorised. There was no accommodation in poor bombed Southampton, so the men had slept in their vehicles.

We approached Worcestershire that summer's day in the ambulance, through the Cotswolds, and came down that famous Fish Hill into

Broadway, said to be the prettiest village in England. I had never been there before, and stared around me with delight. I got the overwhelming impression of honey-coloured thatched cottages all covered with climbing roses.

Little did I think that nearly thirty years later I would be leaving Kidderminster to come and work in Broadway.

The nurse, who had been so kind to us, first doing night duty with my father, and then helping me with both parents by day, came with us. She was anxious to reach England too, and travel permits were not being issued in a general way. I was more than happy to have her with us, as both my parents were somewhat frail.

Actually, the poor nurse was not a great deal of help on the journey, as she felt sick in the ambulance and had to ride in the estate car. Then she dropped my father's urinal and broke it, which necessitated a stop in a town to replace it, which was not easy with our cavalcade!

She more than made up for this when we eventually arrived, except that she was inclined to break all my Aunty Phil's best china. However, she was so nice and we had been through so much together, all was forgiven, and she stayed some weeks with us which gave me a marvellous chance to catch up with all my lost contacts.

My sister had had a weary and anxious time and was very thankful to see us. But she was heart-broken that we had decided to leave Jersey. We had repeatedly mentioned the possibility in Red Cross letters, but she said she had not taken it in. So when she heard our decision was final, it came as a terrible shock. She had been just living to returning home to Jersey. It was a shame for her and we were very sorry she felt so badly about it.

We stayed for a week with Uncle Reg and Auntie Phil. It was nice learning to know my younger cousins, the three girls, who, in age, had followed a long way behind the rest of our generation.

I had only met Little Mary once. She was so-called because she was by far the littlest and youngest of the four Marys in the family at the time. Mary must have been about four years old when I was staying with her parents for a family wedding. She followed me about asking plaintively, "When are you going, Aunty?" She has never been allowed to live this down. She now insists that she was only anxious to know that I *was not* going! A likely story but well tried!

My cousin, Pam, was training to be a physiotherapist in Birmingham. Ann, the middle sister, was at school at, Malvern Girls'

College. Little Mary was at a small day school next door to her home.

We were able to buy a house within a week of arrival though we had heard a lot about the housing shortage. My uncle's firm of Doolittle and Dalley handled the transaction for us. It did not seem to be so complicated in those days, as it is now. Our house was in rather a nice part of Kidderminster. It was situated in a tree-lined cul-de-sac that led to the golf club. It was a very suitable house for an invalid because it had two downstairs bedrooms and the bathroom was downstairs as well.

We had to wait three months for our furniture from Jersey. My Uncle Bob and Aunty Win, my mother's younger sister, gave us marvellous hospitality for which we were very grateful.

Aunty Win had wired as soon as it was possible: "Welcome to Sandbourne as soon and as long as you like," which was very heart-warming. I think it was the same aunt who had telegraphed to my mother on her sixtieth birthday, a day or two before the arrival of the Germans. The telegram ran simply:

"Sixty glorious years," and was followed by the names of every single member of the family. My mother and aunty Win were very fond of each other.

Sandbourne, in its heyday, before 1914, I suppose, boasted an indoor staff of servants of about a dozen and nine gardeners. Gertrude Jekyll, the famous Victorian landscape gardener, had designed one section of the garden. It was hidden behind a rosy-red brick wall and one entered it through a beautiful wrought-iron gate. She had arranged a series of terraces, linked by wide shallow flights of steps. Some of the terraces had rose pergolas, some had little water gardens. It was full of interesting rare plants and shrubs. It must have been heavenly when it was kept in order. Uncle Bob did a little gentle pottering in the Jekyll Garden, otherwise it was left to itself and reminded me strongly of the *Secret Garden* I used to read when I was a little girl.

The only regular help Uncle Bob had in the garden was a veteran from the first world war, called Sydney. He came three days a week and had been their faithful retainer for many years. Though he spent hours at a time leaning on his hoe, chatting, and he also had a crippled hand from a war wound, he managed to do a prodigious amount of work. The lawns were always beautifully mown and edged. The vegetable garden, which was situated behind a wall across a lane from the stable yard, was a model of precision and productivity. The stables were a delight. The horse-boxes were tiled in green and the floors were paved in an intricate herring-bone pattern. A very nice clock chimed away the hours overhead. The horses that once lived there must have been very happy!

Sandbourne House was a gracious mellow building. The rooms were immense but beautifully proportioned. There were two vast elegant staircases in polished oak, uncarpeted and unspoilt. It was lovely in summer but decidedly cold in winter. The old staff quarters had been converted into two comfortable small houses.

Years later, when my uncle went permanently into a nursing home, the whole place was razed to the ground and dozens of little boxes sprang up over the lawns and gardens. Only the stable block was spared and they were converted into several charming little homes.

My uncle and aunt placed an enormous ground floor room at my parents disposal which was very suitable and comfortable. The polished wood-block corridors were so spacious that my father could be wheeled all round the ground floor in his wheelchair.

I took off as soon as they were settled, and first visited my college friend, Jean, who had married a G.I. and was awaiting her first baby. She and her husband were very much in love, but Jean's father was bitterly opposed to the match which made Jean very unhappy.

She had been married in a registry office with two passers-by as witnesses. They had a one night honeymoon at the Cumberland Hotel. This was in stark contrast from her sister's wedding when she married her father's partner. This was just before the war, and they had a marquee on the lawn with bridesmaids and flowers and champagne flowed like water.

Mr. Thompson died soon after Jean was married and as soon as her baby was born she went home to her mother to wait the day when the G.I. brides were taken back to U.S.A.

I then went to London to look up an old schoolfriend of mine who had married someone in the diplomatic service since I had last seen her. She struck me dumb by assuring me she had had a "good" war. I had not realised that any one could have enjoyed it.

I have recently come across some superb thrillers she has written based on her life in diplomatic circles. I do not much care for thrillers as a rule but these stories are so well written with such interesting and authentic background that I found them absorbing. She wrote under her maiden name which is Palma Harcourt.

My next trip was down to Somerset to renew my friendship with my Guernsey landlady and her husband, Adele and Gerry Fooks. They had evacuated in 1945 but eventually returned to the island. They had had another baby, much to my astonishment, and also, I think, to theirs! There must have been at least sixteen years between their eldest and their youngest.

They gave me knews of my other Guernsey friends, Pip and Joan Meadows, who were running a farm in Cornwall, so I hastened down there, to see them. They had had two more sons, following the one I knew about who was born in Guernsey in 1938.

The Meadows's started me off with my first godson. Jean presented me with my second the same month. Clarice Mary Alice Harris, the young friend from wartime Jersey days called my first goddaughter, Charlotte Elizabeth Frances Mary. I suppose she felt she ought to carry on the tradition. She went even further with her two other daughters. With the exception of royalty, I have never known children rejoice in so many christian names. In all, I collected six godchildren over the years.

The war in the Far East was suddenly terminated in August 1945, speeded up by the use of the atomic bomb.

Most people thought with grateful relief that now we would not have to invade in the Far East, and waste millions more lives fighting yard by yard with the fanatical Japanese.

I shall never forget how upset was my father. He said that splitting the atom was the most terrible thing that had ever happened to the human race. He foresaw the most unimaginable horrors for future generations. I was dumbfounded by his attitude at the time. Nowadays, living on the knife-edge of nuclear war, I cannot fail to wonder whether he was right after all. But what would it have cost in lives, money and time to defeat the Japanese by conventional means?

Another thing I remember of my halcyon summer in England was my despair when an ungrateful country turned Winston Churchill out of office. It was the first post-war general election and people had already forgotten the man who stood up to impossible odds in their "darkest hours". In 1940, I shall always believe that God, the R.A.F. and Winston saved us that terrible summer after Dunkirk. I must not forget the indomitable British spirit which always comes out strongest when we have our backs to the wall. They say we never know when we are beaten, and someone else has said we always win the last battle. It seems to me we are not so good at winning the peace.

We moved into our little house near the golf course in October. My sister joined us a week later, as she had had a heavy cold and did not want to risk infecting father with her germs.

The very day Roselle moved in with us, father had a sudden severe relapse. I did not take this very seriously, as I had seen him ill so often. But Roselle knew. Being a trained nurse she recognised the symptoms and she knew he would die that night. This was an added blow to her as she was still feeling wretched about not returning to Jersey.

My father's eldest sister, Aunty Ethel Vaudin, was having a much needed holiday in Tunbridge Wells with a friend, before coming up to stay with us as soon as we were settled in the new house. Her friends were not on the telephone, so we sought the help of the police.

Like our transatlantic cousins, I have always felt that our police are wonderful. Never have I been more grateful, nor has my admiration been higher. It was late on a Saturday night when my father died, but the police tracked down my aunt and broke the news to her. They fetched her next morning and took her to the railway station, saw her into the right train and arranged with the guard to put her into a taxi to cross London. She arrived in the first possible train on Sunday morning, long before we felt we could expect her. My cousin Basil had promised to meet every train from Paddington, and was quite astonished when her indomitable figure appeared on the early train. She was nearly sixty-five then, and had survived a major operation during the war that would have killed anyone less determined. She had started visiting Kidderminster in about 1900, and after we went to live there, visited us every year until she was well over eighty. A very gallant lady.

Her two sisters both came to see us once, but they never came again. They did not take kindly to the industrial Midlands!

My father's death, just as we were settling into our new home was a heavy blow to mother. She took a great interest in the garden and of course it was grand for her to have all her relations around her.

Aunty Ethel stayed with us for six months. She had to undergo another nasty operation during this time. I took her into the Queen Elizabeth Hospital in Birmingham which was quite a jaunt by public transport. She had suggested we need not visit her at the weekend. We agreed to this, but I glanced back through the ward window when I was leaving her, and though she did not see me, I saw the tears streaming silently down her cheeks.

When I got home I said to Roselle and mother, "Come hell or high water, some of us must go to Birmingham on Sunday. She looked so pathetic I could have wept myself."

They both agreed at once and we made elaborate plans to get to the hospital by 2.00 p.m. I think it meant catching four buses. I know we had Sunday dinner about 11.00 a.m. and Roselle set of with our mother. Aunty Ethel was so thrilled to see them. It was a great ordeal for her being so far from home.

It was rather a hard winter that year and the pools that lay just beyond the golf course froze hard. Aunt Ethel and I had never seen ice before. It was a new experience for her to walk about amongst the skaters, and she was always avid for a new sensation. I had borrowed some skates and ventured my luck.

Basil said to me, "There's nothing to it. All you have to do is strike out." He sailed off and I struck out. If I fell once I fell a hundred times. I got so hot I had to keep taking off all my scarves and jumpers and loading them on to Aunt Ethel. I was not a fantastic success.

It was around about this same cold period that I met Miss Oldfield, the head mistress from the high school, when we were both struggling through a blizzard.

"Oh, Miss Oldfield," I said, "Isn't this snow dreadful? I do hate this weather."

Miss Oldfield never held a conversation with you. She addressed you like a meeting.

"It isn't so much the snow," she told me. "It's the attendant problems." She was so right, and I have never seen a snowflake since without remembering Miss Oldfield.

That year, twenty of us sat down to Christmas dinner at my Uncle Reg's house and we were all more or less related. It is sobering to think that in 1974 I was the last one of us left in Kidderminster, and I also left later that year.

In the natural course of events most of the older generation had died, and the younger ones have spread their wings. The two elder Dalley girls have flown as far away as possible to New Zealand.

My great-aunt Mary was one of the most interesting characters in our rambling family. She had been matron of King's Lynn Hospital when she caused something of a furore by marrying a houseman. There must have been thirty years difference in their ages.

She always wore a species of matron's uniform, right up till the day she died, well over ninety. It was a specially made dress with a matching apron and she was never seen without her matron's frilly white cap which tied under the chin in a cheeky bow. She had a lovely unlined fresh-coloured face and sparkling brown eyes. When I remember her best, she must have been over eighty. Her step-brother used to bring her on a royal progress to visit all the family in turn. This was usually on bank holidays. How they ever survived these excursions I shall never know, as great-uncle Arthur was one of the worst and most terrifying drivers I have ever seen.

Great-aunt Mary never got out of the car when she descended on us, unannounced. We would all troop out to her. I remember on one occasion my cousin Basil and his wife Joan, and my cousin Rex and his wife Margaret were all at our house when great-aunt Mary arrived. Both my cousins' wives were very tall girls. Aunt Mary had not met them before and she clasped their hands in both of hers through the car window in the greatest delight.

"And whose little queen are you, dear?" She enquired repeatedly, as we took it in turns to circle the car. It was sweet, but oh, the agony of suppressed giggles! By no possible stretch of the imagination could any of us be called "little".

Great-aunt Mary developed cataracts on both eyes when she was over ninety. She went to the eye hospital for the operations, and I believe they had quite a ball with her. Once a matron, always a matron.

Her husband, Uncle Doctor Webster, had been a surgeon at one time and then went into general practice. I believe he was a very clever and able man. I think he must have been in his seventies when he had to have his leg amputated. He only had a local anaesthetic and watched the operation from start to finish. He said it was very interesting!

They had a friend living with them for very many years. She had originally been the doctor's dispenser and receptionist. She dedicated her whole life to their welfare. There is no doubt at all of her devotion to Aunt Mary, though I have a vague feeling that for a long time it was a *ménage à trois*.

Step-great-uncle Arthur was a dear quiet man who ran a book and newsagent's shop in Leominster. He was married to a formidable lady called great-aunt Amy, who would insist on clasping all my Gethin cousins to her bosom and forcibly kissing the boys whenever they met. They used to fly in terror if there was time. I seem to remember they once played a game of "Murder" with Aunt Amy participating. She played with such verve that when it was her turn to be the corpse, they really thought the excitement had been too much and she was dead!

Step-great-uncle Arthur researched all the family before he died and made us all beneficiaries in his will. There were sixty of us! For years we kept receiving small sums of money that stemmed from Uncle Arthur's legacy.

Another fascinating character was Betty Pound though she was not strictly related, she was much more family than the family! She arrived to help my grandmother with her four children under five. Heaven knows, the poor lady must have needed someone. Betty was fourteen when she arrived as mother's help, and she stayed with the family for the rest of her life. My Uncle Reg and his step-brother, John, used to tease her unmercifully. She simply loved it, and would go off into fits of laughter, striking out at them if they were within reach. After some particularly outrageous leg-pulling she would hide her face in her hands and declare, "I *never* heard of such a thing!" No one dared to breathe a word of criticism of the Dalleys if Betty was about. She was up in arms in defence of her family in a trice.

Aunty Win and uncle Bob had an adopted daughter who was at school at the Cheltenham Ladies' College. They took me to a speech day when we were staying with them in 1945. The head mistress was Miss Margaret Popham, who had been my head mistress in 1930.

I went forward to speak to Miss Popham and had my mouth open to say, "You won't remember me," when she gave me a piercing look and cut me short.

"Of course I remember you," she said, "Jersey. Margaret Vaudin."

What a memory she had! It was quite fifteen years since she had seen me and hundreds and hundreds of children must have passed through her hands. She told me that when she felt she could not remember the names of the latest batch of new girls, she knew it would be time for her to retire. When she did eventually retire from the scholastic world, she became one of the original instigators of the Independent Television Authority.

Before Miss Popham became head mistress of Cheltenham, she was head of Westonbirt School, where Little Mary went when she was old enough. The school wanted a portrait of Miss Popham, and commissioned Dawn Cookson, a remote connection of mine, to paint her. Dawn was a pupil of Annagoni, and she told me Miss Popham was a most difficult subject. She had such a mercurial temperament, it was hard for her to hold a pose.

Roselle had been invalided out of the Army Nursing Service and started another branch of war work as Sister in charge of the sick bay in an underground factory near Kidderminster. This gave her a taste for industrial nursing, and by and large she kept to this branch of her profession.

She did do a little private nursing, however, for a short time between factory jobs. She went to Evesham to nurse the father of the friend I made in Guernsey, Joan Meadows. The old gentleman was universally known as "Grandpy Cox" and his firm of builders was very well known in Evesham. Most unfortunately he had had to have his leg amputated.

The first time my sister pushed him in his wheel chair, he was rather nervous. "Steady on, Rosie," he chided her. "*Steady on!* You'll have me arse over tip!" Roselle laughed so much she nearly did tip him out.

Granny Cox was reputed to be a difficult lady to get on with. Joan and I were both a little worried as to how they would all manage. We need not have been concerned. They dealt together famously.

My Aunty Edith was yet another colourful character. She did a tremendous amount of good work and was a staunch supporter of the Conservative Party. At one time she was a county councillor. She was known as the lady who wore the "pretty hats". She dearly loved a pretty hat. Her friendship with my Jersey Aunt Ethel began when they met at school in Jersey, where Aunty Ede had been sent as a boarder. This friendship was the root cause of my parents meeting each other.

Aunty Edith married a carpet salesman who travelled the world for his company. He was a very fine-looking man, immensely tall and with the manners, it was said, of an ambassador. I heard once he had been invited into a harem as the carpets that had been ordered were not satisfactory and Uncle Harry had to inspect them. His life must have been full of incident. These were the parents of the boys who frequently spent their holidays in Jersey.

When we came to England when young, it was a lot of fun staying with this family. To amuse us, the boys kindly allowed us to play with such things as punch balls and they gave us the most terrible horror stories to read. I used to die a hundred deaths going to bed at night, because the light switch by the door was out of order, and I had to cross the room to the bedside light. They had a splendid retainer called Ethel, I recall, who had been with them for years. Ethel had a penchant for making puddings. Sometimes we had seven from which to choose.

I once overheard Ethel talking to the milkman. They were discussing his holiday. It had been a typically bad English summer, but the milkman seemed to have struck some good weather because he was telling Ethel all about being ill with sunstroke.

"You'm lucky, then," Ethel retorted smartly. This repartee kept me laughing for hours.

One of my friends always referred to Aunty Ede as "Evergreen". She certainly never looked her age, she had the same sort of complexion as great-aunt Mary, unlined and fresh-coloured.

When she was about sixty-five she began to be very short-sighted. We all became a little impatient because we thought she would not wear glasses, thinking it was a sign of growing old. She did not tell us until she really could conceal it no longer, that she was nearly blind with cataracts. All my older relatives seem to have been afflicted with this. My cousin Rex, when he was only fifty, also had to take early retirement because of cataracts and detached retina.

Aunty Edith was quite ill when she had the operation on her one eye. I do not think they operated on both at once in those days.

She wept constantly, fell out of bed, and hit the bandaged eye a painful blow by accident. She was given tranquillizers to calm her, but these did not suit her and she became very confused. Among other distressing manifestations, she took a dislike to my mother!

Aunty Win offered to have her to stay at Sandbourne if a nurse could come with her. We were told that private nurses were a breed extinct in England at that time so my mother instantly offered to send to Jersey for a nurse. Which she did. Unfortunately Aunty Ede took a dislike to her, too! Poor Aunty Win had a terrible time trying to keep the peace.

Happily everything resolved itself in time, though Aunty Edith's eyesight was never very good. I do not think it was ever suggested that the cataract should be removed from the other eye which gave her no sight at all. She eventually developed glaucoma in the blind eye and she was told at the eye hospital that they were going to take it out. Aunty Ede immediately discharged herself, and I never heard that the eye ever gave her any more trouble.

She had a number of grandchildren, none of whom were allowed to call her Granny. She was known to them all as Aunty. We were not too sure of her exact age but Uncle Reg thought her eightieth birthday was looming up over the horizon and he ventured to discuss this with her.

"I'd like to give you a really big party, Ede," he said to her one day.

"What would you like? A midday drinks party followed by a luncheon? Or would you prefer an evening party?"

Aunty Ede had thought about her birthday, I think, and there was no hesitation about her reply.

"It's very kind of you, Reg, but I don't want a party. Please don't tell people I am eighty. If they find out I shall have to resign from all my committees," she said.

My mother had been diagnosed as a diabetic just before the war, but what with one thing and another she had never had much treatment until we came to England.

She had a most extraordinary hatred and fear of injections, which was quite out of character. I lived in constant apprehension that the specialist would prescribe insulin. He managed to keep her stable with diets. This meant she had very few pleasures of the table allowed, except at Christmas, when he always told her to forget her diet.

I once asked him, "Is there no way my mother could have insulin orally?" He explained it was not possible.

Today there are countless preparations on the market in tablet form which would have made her last years much easier and happier. She was the only one of her generation to escape cataracts for which we were very grateful.

I kept house for my mother and Roselle for nine years. I did a lot of jobbing gardening for my uncles, assisting them in their big gardens. This was very useful for pocket money and I also did some baby-sitting.

I was invited to address various ladies' groups such as the Inner Wheel and Women's Institute on my experiences during the war. I was rather bitter at that time and used to tell them a little story about the magnanimity of the British army compared with myself.

"As the Germans were rounded up after we were liberated," I told them, "Some of them were made to clean up some of the places they had requisitioned. I was wandering around the town, and noticed a crowd around one of the hotels and drifted over to see what was happening. The Germans had been formed into a chain and were passing out buckets of rubbish. One or two in the crowd began to shout and jeer but that didn't last very long. A British officer appeared from nowhere and strode forward with his hand held up. 'Stop that,' he called out, 'None of that! The British don't taunt a defeated foe.' He was very stern with us which I thought was a bit hard. I was torn between pride at belonging to such a highly-principled country, and genuine pique that we were not allowed to relieve our feelings in such a very mild way."

Each spring I went down to join Pip and Joan Meadows on the farm in Cornwall which had reverted to flowers after growing food all the war years. I took up my old job again, that I had enjoyed so much in Guernsey, of supervision in the flower sheds and packing the daffodils, narcissi, and tulips in boxes for market. We did not keep the long midnight hours that we used to work in Guernsey. The flower train left at 4.00 p.m. for Covent Garden. Every one in the Midlands thought it sounded like an idyllic Cornish Rhapsody, working on a flower farm in the spring. It was very satisfying but very hard work. I can remember with no pleasure being very cold and very wet with a pain like a red-hot knife between my shoulder blades from standing. I can also remember the good days when everything went according to plan and we had a lot of fun.

I caught measles one year and thought my last hour had come. I felt awful because poor Joan had to take my place in the flower shed. The doctor who was summoned to see me, asked me if I was a virgin, which quite shook my composure. If I had not been feeling so ill I would have asked him what on earth he meant! As it was, I weakly gathered my blankets about me and prepared to scream for Henry, who was the eldest boy and about ten, who was looking after me in the absence of his mother! I have never understood why the doctor asked that question.

Back in Kidderminster, we had discovered that an old friend of ours was X-ray sister at the Queen Elizabeth Hospital, Birmingham. Frances used to spend many of her weekends with us, which was very pleasant. She was very fond of my mother, and we had all been very fond of her mother.

Clarice Mary Alice was also a frequent visitor. She, too, was devoted to my mother and when she married, she gave her daughter my mother's two names besides two others. Clarice had taken up nursing and was training at the General Hospital in Birmingham. She reminded me so much of Jean because she could always make me laugh. They were both natural blondes, too.

My Uncle Reg and Aunty Phil had their pleasant family group disrupted during the 1950s by their eldest daughter deciding she would like to emigrate to New Zealand for two years. My uncle, I remember, said he would not help her to go, but would be more than willing to help her return, if she was not happy there.

Pam has tremendous guts. She was an exceptionally shy child but by sheer force of character has been able to overcome her shyness and has performed many public activities. She went out to New Zealand on an assisted passage. I think there were six others in her cabin.

Also on the boat was a very pleasant clergyman, a New Zealander, returning home after working in this country, Everybody who met Peter said they were much struck by his outstanding ability and character.

Pam, too, was apparently impressed. She came home after her two years was up, only to return to New Zealand and she married Peter in 1956.

Peter, in the course of time, became Bishop of Nelson, when he was still quite a young man. He was such a fine man this was a foregone conclusion. Pam was a magnificent support to him in every way. They have a boy and a girl.

Ann, the second daughter, went out to see her sister when the first baby was on the way. She saw fit to fall in love with a New Zealand farmer and, like Pam, came home to choose a wedding dress and returned to marry John in the South Island. At least Ann had a sister and brother-in-law at her wedding. Pam had no one of her own family at all. I think they were both very brave.

Naturally having two daughters on the otherside of the world changed Uncle Reg and Aunty Phil's holiday habits. Every two or three years they used to set off in October for six months' visit. They went by sea and thoroughly enjoyed ship-board life. They also very much enjoyed missing the English winter and revelled in basking in three summers in a row.

After my uncle died, Aunty Phil continued to go out to see the families in New Zealand but prefered to fly. Partly because passenger shipping seems to be a thing of the past, and partly because she had more time out there if she travelled by air.

At the time we undertook our great removal, my mother's step-brother John was living the old family home, the "Cedars". He was married to another Mary, and had started his family.

The "Cedars" was a lovely house for children. We used to love staying there when we came up from Jersey for holidays. It had very colourful formal gardens, which included a tennis court, a folly, a summerhouse and goldfish pond with a fountain. My mother's step-mother was keen on poultry and she had an exciting area at the bottom

The Cedars, Kidderminster.

My Mother's home prior to 1912.

of the garden for her hobby. Picking up the eggs was a treat we looked forward to. My grandfather kept pigs and these were housed beyond the poultry yard. Beyond that was an orchard. All these big gardens were much appreciated by children brought up in a small suburban home, allbeit it was at the seaside.

The house was low and white. It had an elegant porch where countless family groups had been photographed. The rooms were spacious and comfortable. There was a gorgeous nursery on the ground floor, down two steps. I have never forgotten John's beautiful fort. I did admire it!

John and his sister Ruth were older than we were but were very patient and kind to us. John had a marvellous sense of humour and was very good company. His life ended tragically which upset us all very much. He took his own life in a moment of acute depression when he thought he was in financial difficulties. He was planning a political career besides running the family corn and seed business. He left Mary with four young children.

His sister Ruth caused us some excitement. When she was about forty she decided to get married and went to live in Birmingham. She was greatly missed in Kidderminster where she had a very full life.

She was personnel officer in a big factory. She was the leading light in the local Amateur Dramatic Society. Indeed her performances were professional standard. Their society was interesting in that they were the only group of amateurs in the country to own their own theatre. Ruth was also very highly placed in the St. John Ambulance.

Just before my mother died in 1954, we heard with some surprise that Ruth, who was well over forty, was expecting a baby. It was quite a surprise to Ruth, too!

Roselle went to see her in the maternity hospital and said that the child was the most beautiful baby she had ever seen. Ruth had a very hard time later because her husband became an invalid. Looking after him and the baby, Frances, was a most exhausting business.

The winter of 1953/54 saw my mother's health deteriorating. She was in her early seventies and had never really recovered from her experiences during the war. Though she was up and about every day, it was plain to see she was far from well.

I used to help Aunty Phil with her fund-raising organisation for Cancer Research. She ran a campaign regularly and had collected thousands of pounds over the years.

It happened that we were in the throes of yet another campaign when my mother had a stroke. She had agreed to stay in bed that morning. I was out with Aunty Phil, but was going to help mother get up when I returned around midday.

I had never seen anyone with a stroke before but I seemed to know by instinct. I rang my sister at the carpet factory sick room and she arrived in a matter of minutes and confirmed what I feared. She and the doctor both assured me that my mother would live for some time but she would be a helpless invalid.

In spite of what they both said, I knew she was going to die. She lived thirty-six hours. I was very grateful to a kindly providence that she was not forced to spend the rest of her life broken and crippled.

It seemed very sad to me that she had struggled through the winter months, which she hated, to die on a lovely spring day at the end of April. She always used to look forward to the shortest day so that she could start thinking about the spring.

On 1st May she was buried in St. John's Churchyard next to my father.

It happened to be the day of the Cancer Campaign Flag Day (and it was also Aunty Phil's birthday). I can see Aunty Phil now, standing sadly on the steps of the Town Hall, to say goodbye to my mother as we drove by to the church.

My world has been very much dominated by my aunts. I am truly grateful for all the support, help, comfort and sympathy they have given me. Their friendship has been a golden thread running through my life.

My father's three sisters were so good to us when we were children. Dear Aunt Ethel was a tower of strength at all times. I salute her.

My mother's two sisters and sister-in-law helped make our great removal possible. After her death I grew to know and appreciate them even more.

Being such a staunch admirer of "Aunt-ship", I regret that I have never been an aunt myself!

CHAPTER FIVE

A Rolling Stone 1954-1974

I think I most missed my mother first thing in the mornings. When I used to take in her early tea, I would take my own cup along as well. We might hold a casual conversation, or we might have just sipped our tea in companionable silence. For quite a long time I was at a loss to know where to have my early morning tea.

My mother left me the house in Kidderminster and made it possible for my sister to return to Jersey which she had always wanted to do. After a lot of heart-searching and wearying negotiations, arrangements were finally made. We had decided to spend that summer in Kidderminster. In the meantime I started looking for a job elsewhere. I felt that I needed to go away for a while and have a complete change of environment, though I meant to return to Kidderminster in due course.

It seemed that if I could let the house furnished on a short-term lease it would answer my problem, so, with some trepidation, I bruited this suggestion abroad. My next door neighbour, Clare, the best of good neighbours, immediately introduced me to a charming young couple who were getting married in the late summer and wanted temporary furnished accommodation.

Everything seemed to be slotting into place so I redoubled my efforts to find a job I could take up in the autumn.

I wrote to Joseph and Eleanor Mankowski in French West Africa. Joseph and his English wife had kept in touch with us since they visited us in 1946. They now had two children and I wondered if I could have helped to look after them. It seemed to me that the wheel would have turned full circle very tidily, as my mother had been Joseph's governess. However, they wrote back to say they had just engaged a Swiss girl. I think this was really all for the best because I am not very good with children and the climate in Dakar is terrible.

I then wrote to Buckingham Palace to ask if the Queen needed any gardeners on any of her estates. I was not surprised to hear that she did *not*!

I considered going to Fontainebleu where I had some friends in N.A.T.O. who also needed help with their children. I forget why nothing came of this idea.

I tried the Botanic Gardens at Edinburgh. My mother and I had visited Scotland the last three years of her life and I had fallen in love with the country. I was also very impressed with the Botanic Gardens. There was no joy there either, but Kew Gardens offered me an interview.

Aunt Ethel Vaudin had flown up from Jersey when mother died. She had never been in an aeroplane before but such was her anxiety to come to us as quickly as possible she took her courage in both hands and braved the unknown. She had spent some time with us and when it was time for her to return home, we travelled up to London together. I was on my way to the interview at Kew. In the train she reminded me of a teacher who had been very good to me at school, Miss Joan Skues, who had taught P.T.

"You know, I've lost touch with her," I told her. "I'm glad you mentioned her. I'll ring up her home in Beckenham. She may be at home but last time I heard from her she was in India."

Thanks to this casual query of Aunt Ethel's, my life took quite a new turn.

I was offered the job at Kew, working in the arboretum, at a salary of £5 a week. I said I would consider it, but I really could not see how I could live in London on that money. Had I been younger I would have taken the post without a second thought, because working at Kew was a great boost to anyone aspiring to an horticultural career. But I was thirty-seven and passed the ambition stage.

I rang Miss Skues who came up to meet me at the Army and Navy Stores, I remember, for tea. Bless her, she was full of ideas.

"I've got an aunt who lives at Kew Green," she said. "I'm sure she'd have you as a lodger. That would be one problem solved."

"Well, that would be fine," I said, "but I don't really know if I'm all that keen on going on with horticulture."

She looked at me thoughtfully. "Would you consider living with friends of mine and perhaps doing part-time work in a nursery?"

I gathered it was a nursery for alpine plants not a crèche! "I'm willing to consider anything in reason," I replied. So without more ado she set about making appointments for me to meet her friends and have an interview at the alpine nursery at Bromley.

The upshot of all this was I had two more jobs offered me. So, quite by chance I became involved with another interesting and charming family. I turned my back for ever on horticulture and became the full-time housekeeper and chauffeuse to Joan's friends, Doctor and Mrs. Cochrane.

The doctor was a very well-known leprologist. About this time I picked up a book about leprosy and the dedication ran: "To Robert Cochrane, whose name crosses and re-crosses these pages, as he has crossed and re-crossed the world."

He travelled endlessly. To India, Africa, the Phillipines, U.S.A. Wherever there was a single case of leprosy or where there was a colony or special hospital, there would Dr. Cochrane be found.

His wife was rather delicate which was why he wanted a companion-housekeeper for her, because he was away so much.

His experiments, dedicated work and writing had greatly advanced the treatment and cure of this very unpleasant disease. He was a most remarkable man. He never allowed himself more than four hours sleep at night, and he really believed the Lord would provide. He took no thought whatever for worldly security. His three children were all following in his footsteps.

They paid me £20 a month, all found, which, in 1954, seemed to me to be riches beyond the dreams of avarice. I had never lived near London before, and I thought this was a marvellous chance to get to know the place. American tourists had nothing on me! Whenever I could, I was up there with my guide book. I walked miles, and went everywhere.

I took in the Tower and Madame Tussauds, The Monument and the Royal Mint, St. Paul's and Westminster Abbey. I had lunch at "The Cheshire Cheese" off Fleet Street, and tea at Derry and Toms Roof Gardens in Kensington.

In the summer I wandered about in all the parks, Hyde Park, Kensington Gardens, St. James's and went by river bus to Richmond and Hampton Court.

In the winter I prowled round the museums and picture galleries. I liked the National Portrait Gallery best and the Imperial War Museum. The British Museum daunted me by its sheer size.

The well-known controversial character, Gerald Nabarro was M.P. for Kidderminster in those days. He kindly arranged for me to attend a debate in the House of Commons. I was never more disappointed and disillusioned in my life. The few members who graced the chamber appeared to be asleep. I trembled, and still do, for the welfare of this country. God forbid that the proceedings in the House should ever be televised.

Though I am not in the least musical, I used to go to the Albert Hall and listen to the concerts. I liked to sit up by the organ, facing the conductor. I seemed to be able to hear better if I could watch the conductor. I was once in the F.R.C.P.'s box with the Cochranes when Princess Marina came in and sat in the next box. What a beautiful woman she was.

I visited the zoo, too, which I thought was *not* nice. I came away with the impression of a sea of concrete. I recall seeing a Shakespeare production in Regent's Park in the open air theatre which appealed more.

Sometimes I went further afield, for instance to Canterbury and Windsor. And in the winter I would go down to Brighton or Eastbourne. It was lovely walking along the sea front, out of season. All the ice cream parlours and whelk stalls and fortune telling booths were closed and shuttered and I had the place to myself.

Shortly after I went to Bromley, two friends from Kidderminster came up independently, the same week-end, and both stayed at the Cumberland Hotel. I went up to meet them and overheard one say to the other, "Have you come up to London for anything special?"

The other answered "No, I've only wanted to see if Margaret was all right."

"Me, too!" replied the first one.

I was so touched I could have wept. Clare and Cathrine, I did appreciate that!

My cousin Mary was at the Guildhall School of Music and Drama when I was in Bromley. She was studying drama and her father insisted that she took a teaching course at the same time. Mary thought very poorly of this at the time, but has lived to thank her father for his foresight.

I used to meet her quite often. We usually went to the theatre and queued up for seats in the "gods". Then we would go to a Lyons Corner House for supper. Even with my train fare up from Bromley, an evening out only cost about ten shillings or fifty pence! Oh, happy days!

Another friend of mine who was in London at this time was Dorothy. I had known her slightly in Kidderminster and she has since grown into a very dear friend. She sometimes joined Mary and me in the "gods", and she looked so out of place. We felt she should be gracing a box because she had great poise, dress sense and elegance. After she retired from being a demonstrator with the South West Electricity Board, she became, at sixty, a model for the "older woman" with conspicuous success. Very nearly twenty years later, she still undertakes an occasional modelling session, and she always looks just right.

Aunty Win died in March 1955, less than a year after my mother. It was a blow. She had had a cataract removed in Worcester Eye Hospital and was doing well. One morning she was found dead in bed. It was something of a shock to the staff at the hospital too because they do not often have such a tragedy.

I came back to Kidderminster for the funeral and asked the Cochranes to give me two months leave. For one thing my tenants were departing and I wanted to re-let the house, and also I wanted to be in Kidderminster for "Aunt Ethel time" in May. My mother had repeatedly told me that Aunty Ethel was to come for her holiday for as long as she wanted to, and I was anxious not to disappoint her.

Once again everything seemed to dovetail together. Another nice young couple was introduced to me. They were shortly getting married, and wanted a furnished house for a year. This suited me very well, because I felt sure by that time I would be ready to come home again.

In all, I stayed with the Cochranes for eighteen months and was very sad when I left them. They had taught me a tremendous lot and I had met so many interesting people there. Their immensely high ideals and principles took a deal of living up to and was a bit of a strain, but it was a period in my life I would not have missed for anything.

I had no idea how I should next earn some money. I knew I did not want to let the house again. I had had two sets of splendid tenants and did not feel like pushing my luck again. I remember sitting up in bed at Bromley, wrestling with a budget and trying to work out how much I should need to run the Kidderminster house.

Once more the answer came fortuitously one day through the post.

A lady, a stranger to me, but she had met my mother, wrote to me and asked if she and her husband could rent my house because they were building a new bungalow and it would not be ready for a few months. As I had set everything in train to return and live in the house myself, I replied by saying if they wished to share the house I would be quite willing. I told them they could have a bedroom and sitting-room and the use of the kitchen and bathroom until their new bungalow was ready. To this they agreed. When I returned home and told people what I had arranged, every relative and friend in the town assured me I had made a terrible mistake.

Apparently, the lady had the reputation of being very difficult. My heart plummeted, but the deed was done. I comforted myself by saying it would not be for long. As it turned out, everyone was wrong. We got on famously together and they started me on my new career of being a landlady. When the time came for them to move on, they refused to leave me until they had found someone else to stay with me. They produced the professional from the golf club, which was just twenty yards from my front door.

He was a very quiet considerate man and stayed with me for nineteen years, until he sadly died of cancer. This came as quite a shock as he was not ill, or so it seemed, for very long.

I had a succession of young men in another spare room. George arrived at the age of seventeen and stayed until he was twenty-two. He was an electrical engineer, a dear boy, but villainously untidy and could *not* get up in the morning.

"George," I would yell up the stairs after about the fifth call, "If you don't come down this minute for your breakfast I'm *coming up*!" That usually brought him stumbling down bleary-eyed.

I had to laugh because every time I called him he would answer, "Coming, Miss Vaudin." Burrowing more deeply under the blankets at the same time.

Ron replaced him. He was about the same age and another nice lad. He was the assistant golf professional. He had one fault over which I fell out with him periodically. He could not seem to take a drink without causing himself a great deal of trouble. I did not take kindly to him being sick on his bedroom floor, especially as he did not think to mention it. I was on my knees scrubbing the carpet when the two golf pros appeared at the bedroom door. I do not ever remember being so angry.

"Ron," I said, scrubbing more madly than ever, "If this should happen again, you're *out*."

His senior tried to intervene, "It wasn't Ron's fault. The members kept buying him drinks."

"And the same goes for you," I told him unreasonably, "If I have to clean up after Ron again you can both look for new digs."

They fled from my fury in terror. I could not help laughing. They looked so deflated. I had Ron five years, too. When he did not come for his breakfast, I would go in and see what was the matter.

"I feel ill," he would mumble.

I would give him a long, hard look and then enquire with some irony "Self-inflicted, Ron?" He would nod, avoiding my eye. "Well, get better the best way you can," I would retort brutally, and give his bedroom door a hearty slam for good measure. I cannot think how it was he did not walk out!

I had a long procession of High School teachers in the big bedroom I had rigged up as a bed-sitter. The High School was only around the corner which was convenient. These girls rarely stayed more than a year or two, because they soon left to get married. I think I had three of them who stayed over five years.

Another time I had the captain of the golf club as a paying guest. He was a very pleasant man but a great deal older than my usual intake. Poor chap, he left me when he had to have his leg amputated.

His place was taken by another older man who was no trouble at all and very easy person to have around. He spent a lot of his time at the golf club. He was with me about seven years, I think. I found him other digs near at hand when I moved in 1974. I felt rather sad about these older men. It seemed awful to me that they had no real place to call home.

My house was pretty elastic. When I had my own visitors, I gave them my own room and camped out on a divan in the dining-room. So well were my P.G.'s trained, that often my visitors never met any of them for the duration of their stay. I always said that we ran on parallel lines.

As I only gave the men breakfast, and the schoolteachers looked after themselves, I had time to look round for fresh worlds to conquer.

There was a very bad influenza epidemic the first winter after I returned home from Bromley. My friend, Cathrine, who was personnel officer at a big carpet factory, asked me to help out in their sales office as a temporary measure.

I was not very keen but I thought I would have a go. I was put on to sales statistics of all things. Mercifully they gave me an adding machine. It was quite interesting, in a way, and I stuck it for six months. I found it both tedious and tiring sitting at a desk from nine till five. I had a good excuse for leaving because I wanted to help look after a neighbour who was dying of cancer. I cannot say I got any satisfaction out of this unhappy assignment. She died in April and I was so exhausted I took the summer off and had an enjoyable time with Aunt Ethel and other visitors in my elastic house.

Aunt Ethel was a remarkable lady. She enjoyed everything. She loved to take me out for little treats. I had no car in those days but we dealt faithfully with every place of interest within sixty miles of Kidderminster. She was by this time in her middle seventies, but we sallied forth daily by public transport. She was indefatigable.

I felt we personally supervised the building of the new Coventry Cathedral. For years we paid an annual visit to inspect the progress.

We went to a glass factory at Stourbridge and watched the blowing of the glass and the decorating. We went to the porcelain works in Worcester and saw the process from start to finish. We went to Cadbury's in Birmingham and spent some hours with the chocolate makers.

There was no stately home in the vicinity that we had not visited. If royalty happened to be in the area, we were there! I remember Winston came to Worcester once. Aunty Ethel and I were in the front row!

She was a marvellous needlewoman and knitter. Shamelessly, I used to save up all my mending when I knew she was coming, and she would sit happily for hours sewing on buttons and darning. I can always remember her sitting ready with hat on, about an hour before we needed to set forth on an outing, knitting non-stop. This was called "filling in time". She could not bear to be idle for a moment.

She liked nothing so much as to feel she was being useful. One year when she was in Kidderminster, Aunty Phil was running one of her cancer research campaigns. All the pubs in the town had been issued with collecting boxes. There were over one hundred and Aunty Ethel was sent out with my cousin Mary to drive her, to gather them in. She had been a teetotaller all her life and she laughed until she cried over the idea of visiting one hundred pubs in one morning.

There was a further influenza epidemic the next winter, and I was asked to help out at another carpet factory for a fortnight. I stayed three years. Obviously I liked it better than the first office job I had, but I still felt it was all an awful waste of time. This time I only worked in the mornings so it was not quite so boring. I started as filing clerk which I quite enjoyed. I liked creating order out of chaos, because there was a terrific backlog. Then I was promoted to the wages office. When it was suggested that I should work full-time and do P.A.Y.E., I knew it was time for me to go.

Which reminds me of the old adage, "She was a good cook, as cooks go, and as cooks go, she *went*."

I thought to myself, "Surely there must be a worthwhile job somewhere for a strapping able-bodied woman to do?" So I tried the hospital, thinking there might be someone extra needed in the almoner's office.

They had no use for me, but said, "They are desperate for help in the geriatric wards. Get a doctor's certificate and you can start at once." I recoiled in horror.

They brushed aside my protests that I had no training or experience and would be a menace on the wards.

"You'll soon pick it up," I was assured, so before I knew where I was I found myself enrolled as a nursing auxiliary. Wearing a yellow ill fitting cotton overall with a little white cap skewered squiffily to my head, I found myself entering a male geriatric ward for the afternoon shift. We worked 2.00 p.m. to 8.00 p.m. six days a week and they called it part time!

Had I had my wits about me I would have realised that immediately after their midday meal the patients would be taking a nap. To my untutored eye, as I cast a wild glance round the ward, I was convinced they were all dying, if not already dead. It took a considerable effort of will not to run screaming from the ward.

I was just getting to grips with some of my indescribable duties and getting used to the extraordinary characters I had to work with, when I was moved to another ward. I was beginning to know and get fond of the patients too.

The sister in the first ward had been quite pleasant but the one in the women's ward to which I was next posted was an old battle axe. Her day was quite ruined if she did not have one of us in tears. But she was a splendid nurse and marvellous to the patients, which, after all, was all that mattered.

That first day I was sent into the cot ward. There were over forty patients per ward, divided into three units, all on different levels. The sluice was another level and the linen room was somewhere else, the whole linked by flights of stone stairs. We used to run *miles*! This particular day, the patients in the cot ward were having a *bad* day. Not one of them was lying down quietly. If they were not climbing the cot rails, they were tearing up their nighties. It was bedlam.

The girl I was working with had forgotten something from the trolley and said to me, "Wait here for me. I won't be a moment." I remember throwing a scared look around the ward. "Wait here? Who me? By myself? No fear. I'm coming with you," I said. How she laughed at me!

I soon got used to it but I shall never forget that first afternoon with those poor old ladies.

I was only really happy on one ward. It was smaller and in the more modern part of the hospital, so mercifully was all on one level. The sister had a figure like a cottage loaf and was a darling. I was sent to her in disgrace because I had fallen foul of the sister of the ward I was currently bumbling around.

This lady had forbidden us to give out bedpans between the hours of 3.00 p.m. and 8.00 p.m. I thought this was wrong and said so and asked her to report me to matron. There was a hell of a row but I did not care a jot. I hoped my efforts would help the poor ladies lying there in great discomfort and distress. But I do not think it did. Sisters are all powerful.

I recall with a smile a little story of one of the old ladies who was said to be sensible enough to understand when she was given Holy Communion.

"Hi!" she shouted after the departing clergyman, "Hi! Young man, come back. I only had a drop!"

When I first went to the hospital no one wanted to work week-ends. They were mostly married women and they said their husbands would not let them. Just before I left, overtime pay was introduced. Time and a half for Saturday afternoons and double time for Sundays. Everyone instantly wanted to work week-ends! But for a long time I had worked both on Saturdays and Sundays because so few people would. One of my neighbours was so sorry for me, he and his wife often fetched me in his car at the week-end and we might go and have a Chinese meal. It was never pre-arranged which made it all the nicer. If Tony could not come for me, he would arrange with Spencer, another neighbour, to turn out. They were *so* good. They never knew how heartfeltly grateful I was.

When I was not having these wonderful lifts the picture was very different. The bus passed the hospital gates about five minutes past eight. If we could manage to escape from the ward a couple of minutes early, we stood a faint chance of catching the bus.

We would charge madly into the locker-room tearing off our overalls as we ran. Hurling on our coats any how, we would continue our wild race, outdoor clothes flying, and burst out of the hospital usually in time to see the bus vanishing around the corner. This, after six hours of battling in top gear, lifting heavy patients in and out of bed and in and out of baths, I really do not know where we found the energy.

I gave up my job at the hospital every springtime. I found it so tiring, I could not cope with the garden or spring-cleaning. Aunt Ethel also came to stay in May so I used to take a few months off and return to the hospital in late summer for a further stint. I did this three years running, then decided that I had had enough. I would not have missed my little experiences at the hospital for anything, but it did make me wish I had taken up nursing professionally when I was younger.

Strangely, my mother always wanted to nurse, but her father would not allow it. My sister did become an S.R.N. but always said she wished she had done something else.

During my time at the hospital I won a premium bond prize and I bought cream cakes for all the staff on the ward. We were *all* in the kitchen, including sister (a nice one!) munching our heads off, when who should walk in but the matron. It seemed odd to me, but matron was a gentleman, and I never got used to it. By some lucky chance there was one solitary cream horn left, so with considerable embarrassment, I offered it to him and explained the cause of the celebration.

I was exceedingly relieved when he co-operated, saying pleasantly that he had not had a cream horn for years. I thought he might have sacked the lot of us!

Apart from my hospital duties, my private life had no set pattern. I saw a lot of my Dalley cousins. When the girls came home briefly from New Zealand, prior to returning to get married, it was Mary and I who accompanied, first Pam to Tilbury, then later, Ann to Liverpool. I must say I found these departures very upsetting. I did feel so sorry for their parents. New Zealand was such a long way away.

In 1959, my aunt and uncle started the first of their many trips out to New Zealand. In 1980, my aunt was still travelling around the world by air, on her own. She was eighty years old.

In the early days they went by sea and the first time Mary went with them. They left their affairs in my incompetent hands.

Mary had finished her training at the Guildhall and was quite rightly hitching her wagon to a star. I think perhaps she felt that something like Lady Macbeth at Stratford might be a billing for her to aim at.

Instead of which, she was offered a part in the B.B.C. farming serial, *The Archers*. She had no interest in this at all and her mother and sister more or less dragged her forcibly to the audition. She was given the part, and performs with great expertise and enjoyment. "Pru Forrest", the gamekeeper's wife, does not appear often nowadays, though they keep her alive by referring to her from time to time. Terry Wogan, the other day, enquired on the early programme, if Tom had perhaps murdered her.

She has travelled all over the country opening bazaars and fetes and collecting money for the National Children's Homes. She speaks at W.I. meetings and addresses at public occasions with great charm and professionalism.

Mary introduced *The Archers* programme to New Zealand when she was there. This caused a slight problem with the English programme as the story here was that "Pru" had been sent into a sanatorium for six months because she had a touch of T.B. The shadow on her lung had shown up when she was X-rayed on the mobile unit. (A little health propaganda.)

All her fan mail came to me and I was inundated with get well cards to forward to her and even a bedjacket arrived with a listener's best wishes! Fortunately she had left me a pile of signed photographs so I dispatched these to her fans with "Pru's" grateful thanks.

I think *The Archers* is one of the longest running serials of all time, To my certain knowledge I have been listening for thirty years.

When Mary went to New Zealand for six months, she was engaged to Richard. In September 1959 she was married. It was a most beautiful summer with continuous sunshine from May onwards. Every week we told each other it could not possibly go on and it would be bound to break before the wedding, but it kept up in fine style and it was another golden sunny day. Many of *The Archers* cast were present, including her radio "husband", Tom.

One summer, before she was married, Mary asked me to go to Paris with her. With no hesitation at all I said to her, "Mary, I'll only get a migraine on you. I really am allergic to travel. Besides, you'd have a lot more fun with someone nearer your own age. I'm too old for Paris!"

The next thing I heard was that her parents thought they would enjoy a little trip to Paris. Neither of them had ever flown so it would be quite an adventure.

However, a day or two before they were due to take off on their short holiday, Uncle Reg did not feel very well, so they asked me to go after all. It was hectic collecting myself at the eleventh hour but we managed it and had a very enjoyable time, though of course, I was laid out flat on my back for one whole day with a migraine, just as I had foreseen.

Our cousin, Michelle, who lived in Versailles, rang us up at the hotel, the day I was stretched out on my bed of pain. Mary took the call in our bedroom, and her side of the conversation ran like this, "Oh, thank you, Michelle. That'll be lovely, Michelle. Yes, very well. Yes, I understand. Thank you, Michelle."

Holding my aching head, I said "What was all that about?"

Mary replied brightly, "I have no idea!" Low as I felt, I could not help laughing.

We eventually went to see our relations in Versailles. Michelle's mother was first cousin to my mother and Mary's father. For this reason Michelle considered herself more English than French. Her spoken English is very fluent but strongly accented, which I find very attractive. Usually Michelle talks to me in English, and I answer in French, but Michelle considers my French accent is positively plebian. Mary said to hear us together was funnier than Morecambe and Wise!

Another Kidderminster character was Elizabeth. She had been Aunty Phil's cook-housekeeper for thirty-nine years when she retired. She never referred to my aunt by name. It was always "'Er" or possibly "She".

A classic example would be, "'Er's down the garding. 'Er'll catch a cold. The garding strikes up, ye know." Another little gem was, "'Er come over all no'ow some'ow," when Aunty Phil felt poorly one day.

If Elizabeth was put out, she used to clash and bang the saucepans about in an alarming way. When I used to work in the garden for Uncle Reg, I would go up to the house for a mid-morning cup of coffee. But if I happened to hear a frightful clattering coming from the kitchen, I would fly for my life and forget about the coffee.

When one of the girls was coming back from New Zealand in the middle of the Suez crisis, Elizabeth became very worried.

"Why," she asked me, "Must Ann come back through that nasty sewage?" I thought this was worth treasuring.

Talking of quaint remarks, my sister overheard the following in a bus queue just before the end of the war: "Us be treating they, as them's served we." The speaker, I think, was referring to the bombing raids!

When I had made my positively last appearance at the hospital, I began to turn over in my mind what I should do next. I thought it might be a good idea if I could do a little auxiliary nursing in people's own homes. Quite a few of the patients in the geriatric hospital need not have been there if their relatives could have had some help at home. I wondered if I could have sat with the patient whilst the relatives had a day's shopping spree or maybe a week-end break. Or if broken nights were the problem I thought I might sit up a night or two a week so that the relatives could have a restful night's sleep. It was all very nebulous, but I mentioned it to my doctor, who thought it was a good idea, and said that her practice could give me all the work I wanted.

However, before I could get anything implemented, I found myself involved in an Old People's Home, just around the corner from where I lived. I was asked to go for a fortnight and stayed about seven years.

It was a very pleasant home. I started off as an auxiliary on the nursing side. Then one day the kitchen staff walked out, and to my amazement I heard my voice volunteering to do some cooking. As I had not a clue how any of the complicated electrical equipment worked, I now knew I must have gone mad.

Another girl worked the mornings from 7.00 a.m. to 1.00 p.m. and coped with breakfast and dinner. I did 1.00 p.m. to 6.00 p.m. We had alternate week-ends off, but the week-end we were on duty we worked all day both days.

I enjoyed being tea cook. The old people always had something cooked and always home-made cakes. In the summer I sometimes made them ice cream for a treat. I think poached eggs on toast for about seventy was the most difficult job to get right. I also liked seeing to the diets. I worked myself up into something of a panic to begin with, but the matron so sensibly told me that cooking for a crowd was no different from cooking for a family—one just needed bigger saucepans!

After a while I went into the office. I enjoyed making out menus and doing the ordering and helping with the pensions and staff wages and rotas.

Night duty was the one thing I did hate. I did not often have to do it and I thought it quite wrong that one untrained person should be in charge of all those old people. They were housed in two buildings, linked by a long glass-sided corridor. In fairness, I must say that trained staff were on call for emergencies but we felt it was as much as our lives were worth to call anyone.

Night duty lasted from 8.00 p.m. to 8.00 a.m. and I never would have believed a night could last so long. Soon after I left, I heard that there were two people put on night duty together which I think is a good idea. The first time I ever went on night duty was a Sunday. I happened to be helping at the Morning Service that was laid on for the old people and to my amusement the hymn was "Through the night of doubt and sorrow." I did think it was apt.

Whilst I was working at the home, my sister rang me up from Jersey to say she had to have an hysterectomy operation. What should she do?

"Come up at once," I told her, "And see Dr. Price. I've a friend whose just had that very same operation and she says the gynaecologist is wonderful."

She arrived in a very few days and Dr. Price, who had known her when she was a nurse in training and he was a medical student at the same hospital in Birmingham, had her admitted to Bromsgrove Hospital, about ten miles away. I remember she was put into a side ward. She had said that, though she was a trained nurse, she did not want any preferential treatment. She was sitting up in bed when I went into fetch her clothes, not knowing whether to be displeased because her expressed wishes had been ignored, or whether to be gratified that her nurse's status had been recognised.

Roselle always said that the operation was done so brilliantly that she did not know she had had one, but unfortunately she developed deep vein thrombosis. This was a pity as she had been doing so well.

They started taking blood at frequent intervals from each arm alternately, she said her seat was getting sore and of course her leg pained her, so when the surgeon came to see her and asked her how she felt, she answered very succinctly, "Bloody awful," and has been apologising ever since.

She eventually went back to Jersey where she felt quite ill for a long time. She then met Charles and they decided to get married. He was a dear man and they were blissfully happy. They both enjoyed travelling, and had some splendid holidays including South Africa, the Caribbean, Gibraltar, the Canaries and every year to Majorca.

Very shortly after I started work at the Old People's Home, my doctor rang me up to ask if I could help them out. Myra, their super receptionist, was going on holiday and the relief had let them down.

"Oh dear," I said, "I should love to have helped. But I've just started a job at the Old People's Home."

"Oh, well," said Dr. Aylward in such a tired voice, "We'll have to think again."

"I only work in the afternoons," I ventured. "Could I give you a hand in the mornings? Would that be any good?"

She sounded so relieved as she said, "The mornings are the time we really need someone. We'll manage in the evenings."

And once again by chance. I started a new career, as a doctor's receptionist, which was to last right up until the time I retired at sixty-four.

Dr. Aylward's name will crop up again and again in the following pages. She is quite the most caring dedicated doctor I have ever met. She could certainly qualify for the title of the "Beloved Physician". She has spent herself in the service of her patients and their devotion to her is overwhelming. I consider myself incredibly blessed by having the privilege of working for her for many years. It was lovely being introduced to people as Dr. Aylward's receptionist, and her friend. I liked that.

The first time I ever remember meeting her was one Sunday morning when my mother was still alive. I had woken up with a very painful thumb. It was stiff and shiny, swollen and red. I thought I must have a thorn in it because I never wore gloves when gardening. I soaked it in hot salt water for a while and noticed a red mark running up my arm. I had a vague idea that this was not very good, so reluctantly I rang up the doctor for advice.

Dr. Aylward happened to be duty doctor for that week-end. It was a three-handed practice then, later it became five. Though I only asked for advice, she said, typically, that she would come at once. She gave me an injection of penicillin and, again typically, said she would stay for a while to make sure the injection did not upset me. She told me to go down to the surgery in the morning for another injection.

She completely cured my throbbing thumb because I do not remember anything more about it, but next morning I had developed a magnificent rash, and felt terrible.

I got on my bike and took my face down to show them at the surgery and discovered I was allergic to penicillin. Very meanly I have never allowed Dr. Aylward to forget our first meeting!

I nervously acquitted myself for the fortnight of the duration of

Myra's holiday, and was very surprised when I was asked to do a regular Wednesday morning, to give Myra a mid-week morning off duty.

This suited me very well as Wednesday was my day off from the Home. I worked one day a week for the practice for quite a long time. In due course another partner was taken on and an appointment system was started. More staff was recruited, and Myra, who had been the original receptionist, and had been there for years, decided to start a family. The doctors asked me to take her place on a full-time basis, and as I was just beginning to think I would like a change, I accepted with pleasure.

I did not like saying goodbye to my old people of whom I had grown very fond, but I was very happy to be going to my new job. The hours were very long and the pressure relentless but I loved every minute.

When Nini was my fellow-worker we had had an hilarious time. She was the senior partner's daughter and the most beautiful girl I have ever seen and the most charming. We laughed ourselves helpless more often than not. I was quite upset when she decided to go off to London to be a model.

Ours was a very popular surgery and we were rapidly out-growing our shabby little old-fashioned premises in Church Street. The doctors very courageously launched out and bought a large old house on the outskirts of the town. They gutted and rebuilt it as a most magnificent new surgery. My Aunt Ruth dubbed it "The Palace of Physicians." A fifth partner was engaged, a second secretary and several more part-time staff, though I remained the only full-time receptionist. I always maintained, and still do, that the job is much easier and more satisfying if one is there all day, every day!

A steady nucleus of four regulars manned the two hatches and four telephone lines. There were two girls on the appointments line, and my friend Wake and I dealt with the main line, the ex-directory, and the repeat prescription line. In all, they never stopped ringing, as often as not, all together.

Wake was one of those people who always looked elegant, cool and poised whatever the pressures. She was always beautifully dressed, groomed and correct. So, one day, when she suddenly came out with some horrific language, it took us by surprise, and it took us a minute to get over the shock. When we did, we laughed so immoderately work pretty well ceased.

Two metal filing cabinets fell to the floor with a deafening clatter, and there was a hideous pile of mixed-up medical folders on the floor.

Wake was speaking on the telephone. She covered the mouthpiece and glanced over her shoulder at the mess. Into the silence her clear crisp voice sounded, "God damn it! Bloody hell and *bugger* it!"

The packed waiting-room erupted with laughter. We all fell about helplessly. The doctors came hurrying down the corridor to see what all the noise was about but none of us could speak.

We had a lot of laughs. I remember more than once hearing myself insisting, "But how *old* is the two-year-old?" and then having to apologise to the bewildered mother.

I liked the patient, too, who came in and asked for a repeat prescription, as he was suffering from "Ruddigore". I looked at him fixedly while I tried to think.

"Do you get giddy turns?" I asked him and he agreed that he did. So I thankfully wrote down "Vertigo"!

Another time Wake and I became hysterical when Wake was trying to find out if a patient was on the telephone.

"Are you on television?" she asked hopefully, then realising what she had said she reeled away, helpless, leaving me to cope with the patient and my giggles, not very well stifled.

Two more of my very good friends, Mellie and Pricey worked together marvellously on the appointments desk. I used to call them Gert and Daisy. They were dears, very good to the patients and excellent at their job. I wish all the public who call doctors' receptionists "dragons" could have met our team. They would have soon changed their tune.

I first met Pricey through a lost library book. I had left it at Jersey airport and naturally waved it goodbye for ever. One day a lady rang me up to say her daughter worked at the airport and had sent the book to her mother as she saw it was from the Kidderminster public library.

Amazed and grateful I said, "But how did you find me?"

Pricey, full of apologies, answered, "I hope you don't mind but there was a bookmarker and we looked at it and saw it was your phone bill. It gave us your number."

Mellie was my dear neighbour and I did miss her so much when I moved away. I can remember how her husband, Stan, made me laugh. I did not know them very well and one day I was talking to them in the garden when Stan offered me a cup of tea.

I politely refused and he said, "Oh, come on in, bugger the expense!"

At the surgery we became very expert in noticing the doctors' individual little ways. Most days a patient would come in after the morning surgery was over and the doctors would be trying to get away on their house calls. Usually the patient wanted a document signed on the spot, or a repeat prescription immediately. It was always the same story, he had been unable to reach the surgery earlier and he was unable to come back later and he needed whatever it was *now*.

Unwillingly and with our hearts in our mouths, we would hasten down to the doctors' common room. Each one reacted in his own individual way.

Dr. Price, the senior partner, would sigh, reach into his breast pocket for his glasses, look at us more in sorrow than in anger, and sign the wretched thing we held out to him. Gratefully, we would tear back to the waiting patient.

Dr. Aylward always helped us, too. But we really had the feeling that our demands on her time would prove the last straw for her. We felt dreadful when we had to bother Dr. Price, but felt twice as badly about pestering Dr. Aylward.

Dr. Walker would mumble and mutter and walk away. One would be left standing with the infernal piece of paper in our hands, not knowing whether he would return or not. He usually did, but it was very traumatic waiting to see if he was, or was not, coming back.

If Dr. Summers simply said, "I don't understand," that was final. At least we knew where we were. It meant he was not signing anything else today!

Dr. Hutchinson was charming when we approached him. He would give us the sweetest smile, agree to help and say, "Just a minute. I'll be back." The next thing we would see his white Mini flash past the window. He had escaped!

One of the worst surgeries I ever remember was one evening when a patient collapsed in his car in our car-park. There were two doctors on duty and a waiting room full of people. Both doctors dashed off to the hospital, the one driving the patient's car, and the other trying resuscitation.

The two receptionists were left with the shocked relatives and a roomful of people to placate. And of course the ever-ringing phones. In between making tea and comforting the poor relatives, one of us had to find time to fetch the doctors back. It was quite a night.

Another time I remember being asked to go and collect an old dear who was prone to shop-lifting. When ever she was caught, the police would ring Dr. Price. Once discovered, she was very crafty and put on a very good act that terrified everyone in the shop. She appeared to turn herself into a stiff board. Eyes closed, hardly breathing, even the police wondered if she was a corpse or not. I had an awful time getting her back to the surgery, the police kindly following my Mini, in case I ran into any more trouble with her. She would make an instant recovery as soon as she was safely handed over to Dr. Price.

I had wonderful neighbours in Kidderminster, Clare and Spencer next door, Diana and Tony opposite, and Mellie and Stan just behind, across a little lane.

I remember once Clare and Diana both had flu and I used to pop in and see if I could do anything for them. When I did not appear one Sunday morning, the girls decided, independently, that I must be *hors de combat*. Which I was, with migraine. They sent their husbands to see if they could help me. I do not know whether the men met by accident or design outside my gate. I heard a lot of shuffling and whispering in the hall, and reluctantly opened one eye to see two anxious faces peering round my bedroom door. If I had not been feeling so awful, I would have fallen out of bed laughing, they looked so apprehensive!

I waved them away and the next thing I heard was a deal of clattering in the kitchen where they were washing up everything they could find. I do not think they dared to go back home until they had done something practical to help!

We had a very bad freeze up one winter and Spencer appeared for weeks at my back door with his jerrycans. I had a water supply, but theirs had been frozen in the road. I quite missed his daily visit when the thaw came. He used to tease me as he said I greeted him each morning with a run-down on the temperature.

"It's hotter, this morning, Spence," I used to say, "Only six degrees of frost this morning. I've just checked my thermometer." I am so thankful winters like that are the exception and not the rule.

My Uncle Reg became ill soon after they came back from New Zealand in 1966. My aunt nursed him devotedly for a year. He needed help in every way, which made what happened a fortnight before he died the more extraordinary.

Aunty Phil had gone down the garden to pick some strawberries. Mary and her two little boys were staying with her. They left Uncle Reg comfortably ensconced in his armchair with a rug over his knees and a bell beside him. They were only away about a quarter of an hour. In that brief space of time, Uncle Reg managed to get up all by himself and disappear.

We searched the house and garden and outbuildings. We sent for the police with tracker dogs. It was dreadful. There was no sign of him at all. Eventually, after four hours frantic hunting, a young neighbour found him. Uncle Reg had walked about half a mile down the main road, trailing his rug, turned into a drive way, and there had fallen in the long grass just inside the gates.

I do not know how Aunty Phil and Mary could have borne it if he had not been found before nightfall. I have never understood how Uncle Reg managed it. Nor have I ever understood why the police and their dogs could not have found him sooner.

During the last week of his life, Mary and I were worried about Aunty Phil because she was getting very little rest. After a lot of persuasion, she let me sit with him at night. I remember it was most beautiful summer weather and the roses were an absolute picture in the garden. I do not know why I should feel so saddened when people die in the spring and summer but I always do.

For some years Aunty Phil stayed on at the big family house with Elizabeth, her cook, and a gardener. She worked hard in the garden herself, and she always said it made her feel better if she was feeling a little low-spirited. When she did not go to New Zealand for the winter, she went to Teneriffe with her brother and sister-in-law. She still left her business affairs in my hands. Mostly this was routine but one winter I had quite a ball.

The gardener was growing older and he really took life very easily all the winter but put on a spirited fury of work just before Aunty Phil came back. I was just about to goad him into action at the beginning of March, when he suddenly decided he was past work and gave notice. On Aunty Phil's behalf, I had been paying him all winter, though he had been doing less than any work. I was very decidedly put out, especially as on the very same bleak winter's day, an electrician I had had to summon, assured me that the whole house needed rewiring and it was too dangerous to leave it for another day! Aunty Phil was in New Zealand and due back in May. I thought Elizabeth would probably give notice too, if she had to put up with electricians in every room. I imagined how pleased Aunty Phil would be if she came home to find no staff left and both house and garden a perfect shambles! However, beyond a furore of clashing saucepans, Elizabeth coped with the rewiring, and by a super human effort I managed to get the garden in order and everything was as usual when my aunt returned. I had even got a new gardener lined up for her inspection.

I made a new friend some time during this period, whom I hold very dear. She has done a lot for me in so many ways. There are not many lady solicitors about, but my friend Betty is top of the class.

She became ill shortly after I got to know her, and Dr. Aylward thought she would not be really better until she had a long sea cruise. Every one began to look at me to go with her.

The very thought of a sea trip at all made me cringe, and the idea of going through the Bay of Biscay in February turned my blood to iced water. Besides which, I had three paying guests, a full-time job at the surgery and Aunty Phil was going to Teneriffe again.

If these problems were not enough, I could not help remembering that Aunty Phil had invited me countless times to go with her to Tenerife as her guest. How could I bring myself to tell her, not only that I was contemplating going with Betty, but I would have to jettison her affairs?

I decided that the whole project was impossible and went to tell Betty so.

She was not feeling very well and looked at me not far off tears. "The doctors say I must go away and I can't go alone," she said.

I steeled myself. "Now look, Betty," I argued, "You must know dozens of people in a better position than I am, who could go with you. I mean, *look* at my commitments!"

"I don't know anyone else," she replied hopelessly, "Who has both the time and the money."

This was too much. I beat the arm of my chair. "What have I ever done," I demanded with some bitterness, "To make you think I am rich and leisured?"

Then we both started to laugh, and we have been laughing ever since over Betty's "rich and leisured" friend. In retaliation, I always refer to her as my "Learned friend".

Of course, I went with her to Teneriffe for a month. I had to fortify myself with a brandy, though, when I went to break it to Aunty Phil, who was sweet and understanding about it.

My friends, Diana and Tony, undertook to look after her house and business while I was away. A friend of Dr. Aylward's took over my job at the surgery. I arranged for my two gentlemen paying guests to have their breakfast at the golf club and the high school teacher promised to keep an eye on everything with my cleaning lady who kindly agreed to come in every day to make beds and shake a duster about.

That only left the Bay of Biscay to organise, and I could not do much about that. When we stepped on to the boat, the Norwegian stewardess took one look at me and said, "You bad sailor, no?"

I agreed with alacrity that I was. She pressed some suppositories into my hand. "Oop!" she encouraged me, jerking an expressive thumb upwards, "Oop!"

I was seasick, even so, and Betty remarked in an interested way that she had never seen anyone turn green before. But far from being carried off the ship on a stretcher, or even being buried at sea, as I thought was highly possible, I really enjoyed it. We laughed so much and had such fun we booked to go to Madeira on the same ship two years later.

About a year after the first cruise, Dr. Price, Dr. Aylward and my Learned Friend combined to launch an attack on me, insisting that I should buy a car.

"I am sick," Dr. Price informed me, "Of seeing you arriving at the surgery like a drowned rat on that bike of yours. It makes me feel ill. It's got to stop!"

I had passed a driving test in Jersey before the war. We had tests in the Channel Isles long before it was compulsory on the mainland.

About ten years after I came to live in England I took another test as my Jersey licence was no longer valid and I needed to drive when I went to work for the Cochranes in Bromley. I managed to smash up Mrs. Cochrane's car and was inclined to give up driving then and there but the doctor insisted that I went on with it, for my own good!

When I returned to Kidderminster I foolishly let this licence lapse, as I had no desire to drive any more, let alone buy a car of my own.

So with all this pressure on me to start yet again, I half-heartedly had a lesson and it seemed so hopeless. I was now in my middle fifties and had not handled a car for fifteen years or more. Besides, I did not *want* to be bothered with it. I was perfectly happy on my bike. I can remember the day I told Betty I was not going on with it.

"Well," exploded my Learned Friend, "I do think you are poor-spirited!"

That did it! I struggled on and eventually passed the wretched test again. I should think I am the only person in the country who has passed a driving test three times.

I have to admit that I am very, very grateful for my Learned Friend's timely remark, I do not think I would have responded to any other argument or persuasion. She applied just the right goad at the right time.

I am very unadventurous unenterprising motorist, but I love my Mini and chug around Worcestershire very happily.

During my years as a rolling stone I often went to London for two or three days. I found it most exhilarating. I used to stay at the Regent Palace because it was so handy for theatres and meeting friends.

I was waiting outside Swan and Edgars, that universal meeting place, one day, when a commotion broke out. Two well-dressed, middle-aged ladies began to wrestle together in what appeared to my horrified eyes, to be mortal combat. We all stood around, petrified, unwilling witnesses to what we gathered was the store detective making an arrest. I thought to myself what a terrible way to earn a living and I felt so embarrassed for them both, poor ladies.

For many years I met "the girls" during my London trips. Dolly and Bill, who had been christened Millicent, were quite twenty years my senior, but they were such fun. How they made me laugh!

Bill was a born impersonator. When she was young, some well-known entertainers met her in Jersey and were so impressed with her talent, they wanted her to join them. She was a natural comedienne. Her father would not allow her to turn professional. In fact, he did not approve of any of his four daughters working, but he did not leave them very well provided for, which seemed a trifle unjust.

When in London I would notice Bill studying someone who had perhaps some slight peculiarity or eccentricity, and as soon as we had moved on, Bill would turn herself into this person and give us a performance.

I can recall one incident when they really had me in hysterics. They *would* argue with those elegant flunkies who are to be found on the steps of the Bank of England. "The girls'" brother-in-law held a prominent position in the bank, and they hit upon the notion of paying him a call. This idea was ill-judged. Instead of sweeping into the bank and being ushered immediately into Charles's presence, we were asked which department he worked in, and that set them off.

"How should we know which department he's in?" they demanded.

My sister (in the middle) and "The Girls".

"You work here, don't you? We don't. You should know where he is."

"But, madam," the poor men protested in chorous, "Two thousand people work here. We can't possibly know them all."

"Well, we can't help that. We don't want to see your two thousand. Just our brother-in-law. You *must* know him."

I supported myself against a pillar and gave way to mirth whilst Bill shook her finger in their faces and Dolly laid a firm hold of their arms and continued to berate them. When I could speak, I managed to ease them away, still arguing.

They could not pass a flower-lady or bootblack without exchanging courtesies. Lavatory attendants held an irresistible fascination. They usually discovered in the course of conversation that they all hailed from the same part of the world or shared a birthday. Old ladies and gentlemen would be armed across the road, and chefs would be summoned to be thanked. If we came across any dogs, cats or horses, some considerable time was spent in caressing them.

At the zoo, if an animal was labelled "Dangerous. Do not touch", they would make a bee-line for it, poking their fingers through the cage and crooning to it. Even policemen came in for their overwhelming attentions.

Taking Bill to Madame Tussauds was another hilarious experience. She would love to turn herself in to a waxwork. People would stand around her, arguing. "Was she, or was she not, real?"

When we went up the Monument in Pudding Lane, they decided that the number of steps was incorrect. I thought the custodian would have a fit. "I counted them, I tell you." Bill insisted. "I can count even if you can't." Oh, dear, his face was a study. They returned to the top of the Monument to count the steps again. Of course, they were wrong but they were quite undeterred.

"The girls" and I always went to musicals. I think we must have seen every musical play in London over the years. We always reckoned to get one more curtain call by stamping, yelling and clapping like mad. If we succeeded, and the curtain went up again, we would beam at each other in triumph.

For some reason that I cannot now recall we went once to the Festival Hall, I think it must have been to see the ballet. They were deeply affronted because the national anthem was not played. There was no way of extracting them from the place until they had registered their formal complaint and displeasure at the manager's office.

Doll has been dead for some years now, and little Bill is over eighty. They were unforgettable.

I once took myself to see *Peter Pan*. I think I was the only adult in the audience unaccompanied by children, and I am sure I enjoyed it more than any of the youngsters. I lived every minute and had a large uncomfortable lump in my throat most of the time.

Usually I tried to plan my visits to London around Chelsea Flower Show in May and my old school reunion in October. This was the English branch of the Jersey Ladies' College, and at some point, against all my wishes,I was appointed chairman.

I was so nervous the first time, I could not even focus my eyes on my notes, let alone read them. Amongst my fellow old girls were important ladies like doctors and head mistresses and matrons of hospitals. There were several ladyships and, at one time, the governor of Holloway Gaol was one of us! I was in the chair about five years, I think, but retired when it became increasingly difficult to travel to London on a Saturday, as I worked at the surgery in the morning.

One of my greatest joys during these years was Mr. Pudkin. We had a plague of wild cats in our gardens in Kidderminster and one, a beautiful, long-haired marmalade cat had three marmalade kittens. We tried all we knew to tame the mother but it was no use. The kittens were easier, and it was fascinating to see them playing together, hiding in a woodpile between Clare's garden and mine. Clare wanted to keep two of them, so we asked the R.S.P.C.A. to come and catch the mother cat and the remaining kitten.

In the course of time one of Clare's cats disappeared. The other spent quite a lot of time with me, though I was very careful never to feed it. The time came when Clare was moving away, and she asked me to have the cat. I was not very keen because I was out so much, it seemed unfair to him. But he arrived and it was heaven having him. Even people who heartily disliked cats said he was nice. And cat lovers fairly doted on him. It was amusing to hear my P.G.s addressing him. "Good morning, Mr. Pudkin, Do you want to go out?"

He was about eleven years old when I found him dead one Sunday morning in the next door garden. Everyone was upset. He was such a friendly cat and so very handsome and good-tempered.

I started to dig a hole to bury him, then decided to telephone the bad news to Tony and Diana who now lived in Bromsgrove, about ten miles away. I usually turned to them when I was in trouble and they never let me down. Nor did they this time. Horrified at hearing what I was trying to do, they said they would come over at once and would I please leave everything to them. They were good. When the sad deed was done we were all nearly in tears. I had had a little party the night before when Mr. Pudkin was in fine fettle and enjoying the usual admiration society. Tony and Diana and Dr. Price and his family were all there and they were all cat lovers. The doctor thought Mr. Pudkin must have had a coronary. There was no sign of injury or poison when I picked him up. I have never had another pet.

Soon after my Uncle Reg died, my cousin Mary's marriage broke down. She was devoted to her father so this was a very bad time for her. She had two little boys and has done a superb job bringing them up. Her mother has always supported her magnificently.

We had been encouraging Aunty Phil to look for a smaller establishment for ages and at long last she saw the house she felt she could live in happily. Negotiations were rapidly put in train by our learned friend, Betty. My aunt's bungalow is semi-rural with beautiful views from all the main windows. Her garden is much smaller than the one she was accustomed to, but big enough to give her much pleasure and joy. Her removal was a mammoth task because she had lived in her old house since going there as a bride fifty years before. For the first time in her life, at the age of seventy-three, she began a new life without any staff, and started to cook and entertain on her own. She has literally lived happily ever after.

Mary and I helped her shed her unwanted possessions. As fast as she and I carried things down to the bonfire, Elizabeth fetched them back. It was an exhausting move and took place in November 1973.

All that summer I had suffered from backache and some time before Christmas I was nearly crippled with sciatic pain. Sitting was agony, but lying in bed at night was impossible. I kept hoping it would go away if I took no notice but it did not. I spent that Christmas with Dr. and Mrs. Price and I shall never forget how kind Mrs. Price was.

She is another natural comedienne and born actress. She has made me laugh so much at times that my face positively ached. I have never known anyone quite so funny and so very kind.

My doctor arranged for me to have physiotherapy and that man earned my undying gratitude for all the work he put into getting me right again. It took some months, and I think I might have recovered more quickly if I had taken to my bed, but the pain was much more bearable when I was on my feet, that I begged my doctor not to put me on sick leave.

I was beginning to think that I ought to look for a smaller house with a smaller garden, when one morning I noticed an advertisement for a lady doctor to take over a single-handed practice in Broadway, that most lovely of Cotswold villages. I thought wistfully how such a post would suit Dr. Aylward, and filed the memorandum in her "In" tray.

She glanced at it when she went through her letters, thought much as I did, screwed it up into a ball and threw it into the wastepaper basket.

She had a particularly bad morning that day. Hours later she came out of her surgery and her mind turned to the thought of a country practice. At that moment, it sounded like heaven. She retrieved the screwed-up advertisement and showed it to her friend and senior partner, Dr. Price, who, himself, was retiring in a few months time.

He advised her to apply for the Broadway practice. Casually I asked her, if she was to obtain the post, would she need a receptionist?

Without further ado, she said she would, so my next step was once more arranged for me.

After various alarms and excursions she was duly appointed, and we were thrown into a flurry of selling our houses.

I had always maintained that if and when Dr. Price and Dr. Aylward left the practice, I would leave too, because they had been such super people to work for I really felt I could not face the receptionist's work without their support. By a strange twist of fate, we all more or less left together, and I did not have to make a difficult choice.

Without any real pre-thought on my part I found myself all set to leave the job and the town and all my friends and sally forth to pastures new.

My second great removal was on.

CHAPTER SIX

The Second Great Removal 1974-1981

I lived for twenty-eight years in Jersey, and twenty-eight years in Kidderminster. To make a tidy full circle, I must then, live twenty-eight years in, or near the Cotswolds. At sixty-four, with the beginnings of the "twinging screws" besetting me, to say nothing of this horrific world full of mugging and violence, vandalism, inflation and unemployment, I am not at all sure I want to live to be eighty-four. There is nuclear warfare, too. Looked at in this light, living to a ripe old age is not a very enticing prospect.

I had already asked an estate agent to take particulars of my property in Kidderminster, because I was vaguely thinking of looking for something smaller. So when Mick Aylward's appointment was confirmed in Broadway, I only had to contact the agent, beseech him to get on with it, and give him a key so that he could take any would-be buyers around the house whenever he wanted to. The only other steps I could take was to put the fear of death into my P.G.s *not* to leave their rooms untidy.

Poor Wake, my colleague at the surgery, broke her ankle about this time so I was extra busy doing my own job, helping with hers, and training someone to replace me.

I never saw the people who bought my house until the day the removal men began to move my furniture. My Learned Friend had negotiated a good deal for me, but then she fell ill. The agents gave the purchasers a key, they were very dilatory in paying me and I had a bridging loan. What with the interest on my loan, it was a very worrying time, until everything was happily resolved.

Looking for a house in Broadway was much more difficult. When I went with Mick to see the surgery and meet the retiring doctor, I saw one I could have lived in, though I would have had to have sold most of my furniture. It was a little old cottage, reasonably well-modernised, "two up and two down" with enchanting roses climbing all over the front. There was no garage or room for one, which was the biggest snag that I could see. The cottage was going to be auctioned some weeks hence, and my agent arranged with the Broadway agent that, if they decided to negotiate a private sale, we would be notified.

They did not get in touch with us, and sold privately the night before the auction. I was very cross about this, chiefly because I had wasted precious weeks, and time was not on my side. We were now in the middle of March, and Mick was taking up her duties on 1st May.

I had arranged to have the afternoon off from the surgery to go with my agent to the auction, so I told my colleagues I was going to Broadway anyway, and I would find a house on my own. They fell about laughing, assuring me that *no one* found a house in one afternoon's house-hunting. I did.

I looked at six. Four were out of the question. One was in the right village but up a rough farm track and was so minute I really thought I would have claustrophobia. The other possible was five miles from Broadway. When I was leafing through the brochures, I had picked out this particular house as one I could *not* live in because the outside looked so unattractive. However, the inside was well-planned, having a garage, a very small garden and faced due south. On the strength of these good points, I more or less told my agent to make an offer. But, in case of being too precipitate, I took Aunty Phil and Diana over to give me their opinion.

They were so extravagant in their praise, I had to hush them hastily. I thought they would send the price soaring up.

I had wanted very much to live in Broadway where I would have been on the spot for the job. I had never lived in even a semi-rural area before, and I was worried to death how I should get to Broadway if we struck a bed spell of ice, snow or fog. In fact, I spent the whole of the first summer worrying about the winter, and I looked at every possible property that became available in Broadway for a year or more, before I finally settled down in Badsey. Nothing I looked at in Broadway compared favourably either in terms of money or convenience with my red-brick hideousity in Badsey, so I gradually came to the conclusion that I was very well placed after all.

I moved from Kidderminster on the last Friday in April 1974. I worked up till the Wednesday evening of that week and on the Thursday morning leapt into Marigold, my orange Mini, to fetch the keys of my new house from the agents in Evesham. My Learned Friend had performed the most prodigious feat in completing the legal side in no time at all.

I thought I had better slip over to Badsey whilst I was near (two and a half miles away) to see if the departing owners had left the carpets and curtains as arranged. I was wandering around the house in a kind of daze when I heard the most startling clattering noise.

Convinced that the house—it was two years' old—had begun to fall down already, I rushed out into the garden and to my surprise found a window-cleaner at work. He swarmed down his ladder and wrung my hand cheerfully.

"The lady next door asked me to call, "he told me." She'd heard you were a lady on her own and the house has been empty for months so she wanted to get the windows clean for you. She's paid me, I hope this is all right." I thought it was so kind, I could have wept!

The removal men had planned to start packing up on Thursday afternoon so that we should have little to do next morning and accordingly make an early start for Badsey. I had arranged to be back home from the key-collecting by 12.00 noon, but had told them where they could find a key if I happened to be delayed.

I thought I would just have time to drop in on my cousin Basil in Hartlebury to say *au revoir*.

"There's an enormous furniture van outside your house," Basil greeted me, laughing heartily. "I've just come from the golf club. What are you going already?"

I was already getting back in the car. "The men have come too soon!" I wailed. "I hope to heaven they've left my bed. I'm sleeping there to night, I hope."

I was in time to save my bed but all the chairs had been stacked in the van, which did not really matter, because I had no time to sit down, I had my breakfast next morning sitting on the stairs.

Dr. Price and Dr. Aylward were giving a joint farewell party that night. Though I was longing to go with Mick Aylward to Broadway, I was dreading parting with my friends. I am perfectly hopeless at saying goodbye. I had made a lot of friends in Kidderminster and my roots had gone deep. To change the metaphor, I am more like a limpet than a lady of uncertain age. I do tend to cling to whom, and what, I know.

In consequence, I was inclined to be tearful and my colleagues, at the party, were determined to keep me from giving way all together, and kept plying my glass. I did manage to say my little piece that I had been reciting for years whenever a suitable occasion arose.

> I dreamed that I stood at the Pearly Gate,
> My head was hanging low,
> Meekly I asked the Man of Fate,
> Which way I ought to go.
> "What have you done," St. Peter said,
> "To seek admission here?"
> "I worked," I said, "for all those doctors
> For many a weary year."
> St. Peter opened wide the gate,
> And gently pressed the bell.
> "Come in and choose your harp," he said.
> "You've had your share of Hell!"

I think it went down pretty well. The other day I changed the word "doctors" to "Terry Wogan" and sent it up to Radio 2. It must have been appreciated because he read it out over the air.

The next day I turned my back on Kidderminster and drove off in Marigold to my new home. I had some splendid help meeting me there in the persons of Aunty Phil, Ruth, Tony and Diana. Tony was kept fully occupied doing vital work on all my electrical equipment. Every single plug had to be changed from round pin to square pin.

We all worked so hard that by five o'clock the van had gone and everything was unpacked and in its rightful place. As a very small "thank you" to my gallant supporters, I took them over to Broadway for a meal.

Aunty Phil had been sweet and understanding yet again when I broke it to her that I was leaving Kidderminster. She had known Mick since she was a schoolgirl, and appreciated her qualities both as a friend and as a doctor.

"Of course you must go with Mick," she said to me. "Her need is greater than mine."

I felt awful, as Aunty Phil and I had done a lot together because of her scattered family. With two daughters in New Zealand and the other over a hundred miles away, I was afraid she might miss me.

I certainly did not like saying goodbye to them all that first night in Badsey, but I was quite excited about my new venture, and I did not dwell on the fact that for the first time in my life I was really on my own. Mick was not due to arrive until after the week-end and anyway she was going to be living five miles away.

My move was completely carefree but poor Mick's was not so easy. The retiring doctor was moving out at the same time Mick was moving in. She arrived in Broadway on April 29th and opened the surgery on May 1st. She was moving from a much bigger house. Both her sons had numerous hobbies and possessions she could not possibly jettison.

I once heard that William Morris said on one occasion, "Keep nothing in your house which is not known to be useful or thought to be beautiful."

These words I had taken to heart and had gone through a positive orgy of throwing away things for which I felt I had no further use. It was excellent self-discipline for a natural hoarder.

Mick's garage was stacked to the ceiling with packing cases that did not get unpacked until she moved again, eighteen months later.

Her house was pleasant to look at from the outside (the reverse from mine), but very small. A waiting room and surgery had been built on at one side and were quite separate from the main house.

Mick had a hatch knocked through the outside wall into the waiting room from the dining-room so that I could have access to the patients. This was a mammoth task, clawing through eighteen inches of solid stone. Never shall I forget the mess.

Mick had to forego her dining-room which was turned into the office-cum-dispensary. This left her with a small living-room for all purposes for her family. The kitchen was small, too, and prehistoric. As soon as she had got her breath back from the trauma of the move, we began to house-hunt for her, because the accommodation was so limited.

The previous doctor had had virtually no ancillary help and kept the patients separate from the living quarters. The practice had grown under her care, and, of course, Mick's popularity was assured. Her reputation for compassion and clinical care was soon bruited about and we were besieged with requests from patients to join her list. I was frequently told that visiting Dr. Aylward's surgery was not like going to the doctors at all. It was like visiting a friend.

There were around 1,300 patients when Mick took over and this figure rose to nearly 1,800 by 1981.

We had a lot of problems to start with as neither of us knew the area or the consultants. There was a G.P. cottage hospital in Evesham but acute cases and accidents had to travel to Cheltenham or Worcester fifteen miles away.

After a few months, having consulted the patients, we set up an appointments system for the evening surgeries. Morning surgeries were left as they were, free-for-all. We also began to dispense prescriptions for patients who lived over a mile from the chemist. Under Mick's supervision, I really enjoyed dispensing and ordering stock from the wholesaler. I am not a secretary or a shorthand typist, but I struggled with the letters and the books and my own P.A.Y.E. I much preferred the personal contact with the patients. I was never much good at the paperwork but it was accomplished. My annual confrontation with the perfectly charming and harmless accountant gave me sleepless nights for weeks.

It was in October, that first year, that Mick brought her old friend, Mary, to live in the already overfull small house. Mick had a great affection and respect for this old friend, who had become too infirm to live alone, but who did not want to go into a nursing home.

Mick put her own bedroom furniture into store and installed Mary in that room, having fetched Mary's own bed and various bits and pieces that would make it "home" for the visitor. Both Mick's two sons were at boarding-school, so when they were away, Mick borrowed one of their rooms to sleep in. In holiday time, Mick slept on a put-you-up in the office, the one-time dining-room.

It was the following May, when we had been in Broadway a year, that Mick was admitted to hospital as an emergency with an impacted wisdom tooth. Dr. Rosser, Mick's predecessor, kindly came to our rescue as locum. The antibiotic Mick was given when she came home did not do her any good and she became more and more ill. Dr. Rosser insisted I called Mick's own doctor who lived some miles away. Mick had some difficulty in forgiving me, because she so hated to give her doctor, or anyone else for that matter, any trouble. She is the most splendidly generous giver but a hopelessly unwilling taker.

She felt so ill she asked me, if she did not get better, if I would look after the boys. This remark, needless to say, frightened me half to death.

Her doctor took a swab, prescribed the correct antibiotic, and eventually she felt better, and, typically, returned to work far too soon.

Soon after this episode, her old friend decided to go into a home, after all. She moved to Bromsgrove just before the boys came home for their long summer holidays.

Mick found a charming bungalow about two miles from the surgery, and moved in just before she went into hospital for a cataract operation in October.

By this time Dr. Hutchin had appeared on the scene. He was a very experienced retired doctor, who lived near Chipping Campden, and he loved to work. Retirement held no joys for him. He and Dr. Rosser took care of the practice between them whilst Mick was off sick.

Dr. Rosser had a splendid helper called Mrs. Smallbone, who used to help her in the house and take phone calls and messages when the doctor was out. She soon became part of our team. The district nurse, Sister James, who had been a tower of strength in the village for many years, became more and more Mick's right hand. I do not know how we should have managed, when we first arrived, without these two, because they were so helpful, knowing the area and the patients.

When Mick moved out of the surgery, Sister James moved into a flat that Mick had arranged for her on the bedroom floor, and we gradually took over the whole of the ground floor for medical purposes.

Being a single-handed doctor on call twenty-four hours a day, seven days a week, is not easy. It was very expensive paying a locum if Mick wanted any time off, other than sick leave. That first year, Dr. Price was still in Kidderminster. He was retired and waiting to move down to Cornwall. He came over two or three times to act as locum to give Mick a break.

"I don't want to be paid," he told us. "I'm happy to do it for the love of Mick."

A lot of us adopted this pleasant turn of phrase.

Both Dr. Price and Dr. Aylward shared that wonderful gift that made each and every patient feel that they were all-important and they always managed to give everyone the impression that time was of no account whatsoever.

In February 1979, Mick had to go into hospital again to have her other eye attended to for cataract. At the time, we did not know, but she did, that she would soon have to have an abdominal operation.

It was May before she told us she was going in almost immediately for major surgery. She had known, since before Christmas, that this was pending but she did not want to worry us by mentioning it.

Broadway, Worcestershire.

"I don't mind the operation," she told me. "The worst part of all has been breaking it to you all."

I do not like to think about that summer. It was something of a nightmare.

We needed locums for at least three months and should have had them for longer. Dr. Hutchin was already booked up as locum to other practices. We appealed to Dr. Handley in Malvern, who had been a magnificent help when Mick was having her second cataract removed in February. It had been a very bad winter and Dr. Handley had slogged over from Malvern, twenty-odd miles away, every week-end for a month through difficult snow and ice conditions. Dr. Hutchin held the fort during the week and he frequently found himself sliding backwards down Fish Hill which was like the Cresta Run the entire month.

Dr. Handley was very willing to help in May when the news broke that Mick was going to have major surgery, but he could not pledge himself to undertake several months continuous work. He enjoyed retirement, and only helped us out now and again because he was sorry for Mick.

Dr. Rosser was also willing to help, and another semi-retired doctor from Toddington also agreed to take some surgeries and night-calls, and of course the visits during the day, when he was on duty for our surgery.

We managed to patch together a rota with these three doctors for the first six weeks. It worked very well, though the poor patients never knew who they were going to see. Not that they minded. All they cared about was how Dr. Aylward was and would she be quite well again soon. Prayers for her recovery were winging their way upwards to the Almighty from Catholic, United Reform and Church of England churches.

The second half of this period had more continuity about it because we managed to contact a New Zealander who came for a week.

Dr. Hutchin was so sorry he could not help us himself, but he persuaded his friend, Dr. Cameron, from Scotland, to come for the whole month of July, and Dr. Hutchin took over the last week himself.

We certainly had to cast our net far and wide. Most of the doctors stayed with me and I became quite used to adjusting myself to the comings and goings of perfectly strange gentlemen.

Mrs. Cameron came with her husband from Scotland and they have since come to live in Broadway and we have become very good friends. I could not resist the temptation to call her Janet, after the lady who looked after Dr. Cameron in the T.V. serial *Dr. Findlay's Casebook*.

Mick recovered and came back to work far too soon. After evening surgery she usually had two or three patients to treat with hypnosis. She had taken some courses before she was ill, and had very conspicuous success in many cases. It must have exhausted her to do this after a long hard day and when I protested she would say, "They need the help. I can't say I'm too tired. I have to help people as long as I am able."

If I persisted she would close the discussion by saying, "Well, we'll see," which was her polite way of saying, "For heaven's sake, *shut up*." I knew when I was beaten.

It was unfortunate that there was no friendly co-operation with the other practice in the village, which was a three-handed one.

Our patients were some of the most delightful people I have ever met. With one or two notable exceptions, they were singularly undemanding. One of these exceptions, I am certain, helped precipitate the illness that finally made Mick consider early retirement.

I seem to have run on at some length about Mick's illnesses. Even so, I have not mentioned three operations on her spine when she was in Kidderminster and polio when a child. To say nothing of the trauma of a broken marriage. Whenever I have tried to sympathise over these misfortunes, she always declares that she is so lucky! *All* I can say to that is, I sincerely hope I never meet anyone who is said to be unlucky!

It was Christmas-time 1976 when my sister phoned me from Jersey one Sunday at lunch-time with the sad news that her husband, that dear man, Charles, had just had a fatal coronary. It was such a shock to her, I really do not think she has ever recovered from it. They always went out for Sunday lunch and he had just reminded her that it was time they put their coats on: with that he dropped down and died.

What with a post-mortem and Christmas it was ten days before we could have the funeral. Charles's daughter lived in Cornwall and she arrived just in time for that and stayed with my sister for a week. I had managed to fly down the day after he died and my sister and I spent a very sad Christmas together. I remember I returned to England on an evening flight and we seemed to be flying through navy-blue velvet. The lights of London were like fairyland. I do not recall ever feeling more exhausted and on the plane ordered a double brandy for the first time in my life.

Jamie, Mick's younger son, had manfully taken my place at the surgery. He had sometimes helped me before so he was not quite a stranger to the routine.

I was still allergic to holidays and insisting it was easier not to have any. Now and again Mick brushed these protestations aside and compelled me to have some time off. A friend who had helped in the Kidderminster surgery came over once for a few days, and two very delightful nurses gave up a week of their holiday another time. This was a great success. One of the girls was a niece of my learned friend, Betty. They took over my house while Betty took me down to Cornwall.

I reached the age of sixty in May 1977 and gleefully started to draw my weekly old age pension, carefully organising my salary so that I did not contravene the law that set down how much an O.A.P. could earn.

It took me a long time to make friends in Badsey, chiefly because I was in Broadway so much. Also, three of the houses in my little row were unoccupied for a long time and two of the families living directly opposite, believed in keeping themselves to themselves. Time, I am thankful to say, has altered all this and I now live in a very happy little community.

I had a vague idea I ought to join something in the village in order to meet people, so I attempted bell-ringing and learned enough to appreciate how difficult an art it is. The skins came off my hands because I kept seizing the rough rope and missing the nice soft fluffy "sally".

In September 1978, Aunty Phil took off for New Zealand again. Her daughter, Pam and her husband, Peter, who was now the Bishop of Nelson, had been to England for the Lambeth Conference and they were all returning to New Zealand together. Usually, Aunty Phil put all her valuables in the bank before she went away, but this particular time she was not quite so careful. Within twenty-four hours of her departure, burglars broke into the bungalow and made quite a haul.

This really upset me because I was supposed to be in charge, though her kind neighbours had relieved me of a lot of my duties and tried to keep their watchful eyes on the bungalow. They were almost as upset as I was. I remember looking round the bedroom and quavering, "How ever are we going to tell Aunty Phil?"

In point of fact, they did not vandalise the place and when I wrote to Aunty Phil I told her that they had been "well behaved thieves". This was a crumb of comfort to me until Mary, my cousin, suggested that they were coming back for the rest! With a furniture van, she added, for good measure!

I spent every available minute I could at the bungalow, trying to find what was missing and making lists for the police and insurance company. My Learned Friend helped me and we hastily installed a burglar alarm. Aunty Phil and I kept up endless correspondence and Mary and I discussed equally endlessly on the phone the various problems with which we were involved. I was working full-time at the surgery and began to worry in case I became too tired to do my job properly. I even felt I might fall ill and then I would be letting Mick down with a vengeance.

Though it was the last thing I wanted to do I decided that the time had come to ask Mick to think about replacing me. I felt terrible as I felt I was failing her, anyway, by proposing to leave her. I loved working for her and I kept thinking of what a dear old patient said, when she heard I was accompanying Mick from Kidderminster to Broadway.

"Arn't you the lucky one?" she said to me longingly.

I *was* the lucky one and I felt very depressed at contemplating the dismal fact that I was throwing in my hand.

Sister James was working as surgery nurse and helping in the office by now, as well as living in the flat. She had been ill and retired from being district nurse. She only worked in the mornings and was a great help to Mick but she was not able to work all day. Anyway, we were so busy in the office in the morning with appointments, repeat prescriptions and dispensing, it was necessary to have two members of the ancillary staff on duty.

A splendid little girl called Sarah was recruited. She was only eighteen, which I thought was a bit young. She was a first-class shorthand typist and had had some business training. She worked with Sister in the mornings, and I hoped she would stay and work the evening surgery as I had done, but this was not to be, so I became that person I had so often sworn I would never be—a part-time doctor's receptionist.

I must say, to begin with, I found it very hard-going and was strongly inclined to burst into tears at the drop of a hat. After a while, of course, I settled down and quite enjoyed it.

Sarah and I shared the responsibility for organising all the aspects of the drug dispensing and reordering. I enjoyed these details and watching our little business grow.

Twice during the seven years Mick was working as a single-handed doctor in Broadway, on top of all her other duties, she organised sponsored walks. The first one was in aid of the Cobalt Unit in the cancer research department at Cheltenham Hospital. Our aim was to collect £1,000 and we finished up with over £2,000. That walk took us over the hills to Prestbury, about sixteen miles. It was a hard walk and I personally only did the first half which was the easy bit!

The idea for the second walk followed a programme Mick saw on T.V. about the starving children in Cambodia. She was so upset by it she felt she must do something to help so off we went on another walk. The leader on both these occasions was a gentleman of over eighty. I blush to admit it, but I did not finish this walk, either. I *might* have achieved it if I had not fallen off a stile on top of Jamie Aylward and ricked my knee. I had some wonderful generous sponsors and my personal contribution to the fund was over £100. This charity did not have the same appeal as the cancer research one. We had fewer walkers and fewer sponsors so did not do nearly so well.

Though Mick did so much good in a thousand ways (I once heard her arrival described as "the best thing that ever happend to Broadway"), she was no priggish do-gooder. When really put out when she was exhausted, she could let rip with some very full-blooded language indeed. Battling with red tape at the end of a long tiring day, I have heard her slam down the telephone with such force it not only made me jump, but caused me to wonder if it had been put out of commission. She has always hated the telephone. She has a wonderful gift with words and can write a vitriolic letter if the need should arise.

Being a Scot, she enjoys her dram or a glass of dry sherry in the evening. Though she is a superb cook, food interests her not at all. She is a heavy smoker and lives on coffee and cigarettes with an occasional apple, banana or piece of cheese. One of her greatest pleasures is doing *The Times* crossword puzzle every day. Her sense of humour is very active and I have seen her laugh until she is helpless. Especially over our "funnies", so-called true extracts from letters to the Department of Social Security. A sample of these letters I have appended at the end of this chapter. For the maximum amount of hilarity, these should be read aloud, to a group of people. Sometimes I have had to stop reading because I was afraid somebody would do themselves a mischief, they were laughing so much.

It was strange, after living so long in Jersey and Kidderminster where, in both places, my respective families were very well known, to arrive in a place where I did not know a single soul.

I remember, the very first afternoon, a nice lady hailed me in Broadway. She was exercising her big dog, and I had wee Fluff, Mick's little Corgi.

"Tell me," she asked in a slightly surprised tone," Are *you* Dr. Aylward?"

"Not me," I hastened to reassure her, "I'm just the receptionist."

Jean has become such a good friend. We laugh at the same kind of things, and I shall always remember gratefully that she was the first person to speak to me in what really felt like foreign parts.

Later on, two very well-known and charming ladies "adopted me". I spent some very pleasant evenings at their beautiful bungalow being fed delicious food. They had run the best tea room in Broadway for many years and were delectable cooks. They had a wonderful humorous outlook on life, and it was very sad when one of them died two years ago, leaving Meggie to soldier on alone. Doreen, who died, had been the business head of the friendship. They had been together for half a lifetime. They both suffered from arthritis, especially Meggie, who, at eighty-one, has just survived her eighteenth operation. She is amazingly courageous and cheerful, and does not allow herself to complain about her numerous disabilities. Her friends are legion, from peers of the realm down to ordinary mortals like me.

In Badsey at week-ends, if I had not gone to see friends in Kidderminster, and if I had no visitors staying with me, I went to church. I had never lived near a church before and the bells called me in. I loved to hear them, even if I could not ring them!

A very kind-looking man, I noticed, appeared at weekends, at the end house of my little row, and spent hours mowing his lawns. Wistfully, I used to pass the time of day with him and I wished I knew him better.

At last I plucked up courage and asked him to bring his wife to a pre-lunch Sunday glass of sherry. It transpired that they had bought the house for their retirement and at present lived in Birmingham. Mr. Seaman was, at that time, vice-principal of a training college, and Mrs. Seaman was nursing at the Children's Hospital. This was my first social contact in Badsey. The vicar had called, I must say, but I was at work.

When the Seamans eventually retired the whole village rejoiced. They have both been a tower of strength and help to everyone, in private and in a most public-spirited way. Esmé Seaman and I also share the same kind of sense of humour. She is a most talented amateur actress among many other accomplishments.

I was asked to join the Parochial Church Council when I had been living in Badsey for two or three years. I had never had any experience of this kind of voluntary work and I found it interesting and indeed most amusing at times.

Another friend I eventually made who has been extremely kind to me is Mona. She used to be a hairdresser, and the poor soul tries to keep my hair in some kind of order. She has an uphill task. I would rather do almost anything than sit and have my hair done. Mona is so patient, in that whatever time of the day or night I suggest, she is always willing to "do" me. I am afraid I do not do her skills much credit.

Mona has a delightful friend called Beth, who lives in a lovely old Georgian house. I first met her over some genuine antique French glass cloches which look literally like elegant bells in the garden. She had a considerable number of them but had decided to part with them though they are really collectors' pieces. Beth, too, has proved to be another congenial friend of mine.

When Mick was ill and I had a continuous procession of doctors staying with me, my neighbours really turned up trumps. They were so upset to hear of the doctor's illness and knew they could do nothing to help her, so they compromised by helping me. I was so touched by their kindness and thoughtfulness.

Joy, who lived opposite, staggered over the road one day with an immense heavy tray laden with delicious sweets to put in the freezer to use as I needed them. Ivy, next door, insisted on washing all the bedlinen and towels for the "duration", because she knew I did not have a washing machine. Elsie, next door on the other side, lent me a bedroom because at one point, I was overflowing with guests. They were all wonderful.

Diana, who now lived in Malvern, rang me up in the spring of 1978 to say, "I've heard of a nearly-new Mini and you are the only person I know who is fanatical about Minis. It's a good buy, if you're interested."

"Whatever do you mean?" I asked her, aghast. "I can't part with Marigold. She's my friend, we've been through a lot together!"

Diana sighed. "I knew you'd say that, but she won't last for ever, you know. She is getting on a bit."

"Well, I'm devoted to that little car. She's never let me down. I can't just jettison her. I have just worked out that she ought to last my driving life, because you know I never drive more than thirty miles from my home base."

Diana could not help laughing at that, and asked how many miles there were on the clock.

"Fifty-five thousand," I replied, beginning to think I was talking foolishly.

"This one I'm talking about has done eight thousand. The owners are doctors who are going abroad. I don't want to influence you, just think about it overnight. I'll tell you one thing, if I could afford it, I'd snap it up."

The upshot of it was that Diana and Tony bought Marigold from me and gave her a good home, and Bluebell came into my life. I had a lot of trouble with her to begin with and came within an ace of fetching Marigold back. But most of her teething troubles were put right under warranty and she has turned out to be as good a little car as Marigold was.

The Fancutts are responsible for my trouble-free motoring and I am considerably in their debt for their care of my Minis. Mr. and Mrs. Fancutt run a small garage five miles away and are consistently kind and helpful.

I am a perfect moron when it comes to the maintenance of cars and I am more than grateful for their patience. Recently I fell on the ice and broke my wrist when visiting my Learned Friend in Kidderminster. Mr. Fancutt drove through flood, fog and ice to bring Bluebell and me back in a breakdown truck.

During the summer of 1979, I had visitors staying non-stop for the whole summer. My sister brought her friend Kitty from Jersey who did not know this part of the world at all so we had to organise a mini Cook's tour of Worcestershire for her. They had timed their visit to be here for the asparagus season, which is a feature of this part of the Vale of Evesham.

Dorothy, that indomitable model for the older woman, paid her annual visit during the strawberry season. We became quite carried away, picking far more than we needed because they were so plentiful and cheap and the site was so delightful, it was a pleasure just to be there.

The biggest thrill was that Jean, my old college friend, came to visit me from the U.S.A. I had not seen her for about twelve years. Elsie, from next door, was wonderful, and drove me up to Heathrow to meet her.

What a frightful place Heathrow is! It was boiling hot and the plane was late. So many people were milling about I wondered if we would ever find Jean. What is more, would I even recognise her again after so many years? After all, people do change, I find, with the passage of the years.

As usual, all went well in the end and Jean and I had a wonderful time and a lot of fun. The weather was that of a typically English summer-atrocious. Jean thought it was heaven because the temperature had been over 100 degrees when she left the Middle West. Apparently it remains in that region for weeks on end. Conversely, in the winter, the temperature drops to umpteen degrees below freezing, and stays like that for weeks, too. I could not help being thankful that Britain is a temperate climate, albeit I grumble about our weather as much as the next person.

I was doing part-time work at the surgery and left Jean to herself from four o'clock in the afternoons. She amused me a lot by requesting "English food". She insisted that the food in the States was not a patch on what she tasted here. She particularly begged for fish and chips (preferably out of a newspaper), sausage and mash and pork pies! I enjoy cooking and had prepared some delicacies which I thought she might like. My chicken marengo and pork in orange sauce had to stay in the freezer. I did not dare suggest them. She also craved for Birds Custard and Marmite!

We toured the Cotwolds with a will and visited about twenty villages and those beautiful gardens at Hidcote. We went swimming a lot in Evesham baths as the weather was so awful, and had countless pub lunches which she enjoyed.

The Trooping of the Colour was on whilst she was with me. It was my Saturday on duty (Sarah and I shared alternate week-ends), and when I came home Jean greeted me with tears pouring down her cheeks, "I've seen the Queen," she sobbed, "I didn't know I loved her so much."

There speaks an exile. Though Jean has collected a strong American accent she is as homesick now as she was when she first went out to the States as a G.I. bride.

In May 1980, Aunty Phil became eighty years old and I gave her a mini "This is your Life" party. I had vaguely asked her to lunch on her birthday, and persuaded about thirty friends and relatives to arrive before her. She was quite taken aback to be greeted by a roomful of people toasting her and singing "Happy Birthday". Ninteen-hundred was a good vintage year for ladies, what with the Queen Mother, my friend Meggie from Broadway, my old comical friend Bill (née Millicent) and Aunty Phil to name but a few that spring to mind.

Between Christmas 1980 and New Year, Mick told us that she had been ill again over the Christmas holidays. She had not called her own doctor, of course, nor had she requested any help from the various locums who lived in the district, because she did not want to spoil their festivities.

This time she said she would *have* to retire. I had been begging her to do just this ever since her second cataract operation and had redoubled my pleas after her major operation in the summer of 1978.

The news that she had finally brought herself to make this decision should have filled me with relief and joy. But knowing her so well, I knew that Mick must be feeling very ill indeed if she were contemplating throwing in her hand. Thankful though I was, I could not help but feel very heavy-hearted.

As events turned out, what with the worry and uncertainty the next few months brought to her, I really thought she might die before her retirement day arrived.

She gave notice on 1st January, explaining that she was being forced to take early retirement on doctor's advice owing to ill-health. Though three months' notice is the norm, she agreed to wait until 31st July, as she was told this length of time was needed to find her successor.

The post was advertised and several doctors came to see the surgery which was all very time-consuming. She was anxious to help obtain the best possible doctor for her beloved patients. After weeks of frustration, and rumours and counter-rumours it transpired that the small single-handed practice was to close, and the two surgeries merged into one.

All this was very upsetting as our patients liked their little practice and Mick had been looking forward to retirement, leaving her patients in the care of a sympathetic new doctor, in the premises that the patients had been used to. From time immemorial, there had been two practices in the village.

She fleetingly considered withdrawing her resignation and soldiering on but knew in her heart her physical strength was unequal to it.

We had been gradually running down our stocks of drugs for some time, and now began seriously to clear up our seven years work and finalise the closing down of the surgery. It had been a very unhappy summer for us all.

Though I was very thankful that Mick had laid down her burden at last, it was with a very heavy heart on the morning of 1st August 1981, I picked up a screwdriver and took Mick's name plate off the gate.

Dr. M. H. Aylward, M.B., M.R.C.S., L.R.C.P., had retired.

Genuine extracts from letters written to the Department of Health and Social Security.

1. I cannot get sick pay. I have six children. Can you tell me why this is?
2. This is my eighth child. What are you doing about it?
3. Mrs H. has had no clothes for a year. The clergy have been visiting her.
4. In reply to your letter. I have cohabited with your officers for a year without success.
5. I am glad to say my husband, who was reported missing, is now dead.
6. Sire, I am forwarding my marriage lines and two children, one of which is in the enclosed envelope.
7. Unless I get my husband's money, I will be forced to lead an immortal life.
8. I am writing these few lines for Mrs. F. She cannot write herself. She expects to be confined next week and she could do with it.
9. I am sending you my marriage certificate and six children. I had seven but one died which was baptised on half a sheet of notepaper by Rev. T.
10. Please find out if my husband is dead, as the man I am living with won't eat or do anything until he is certain.
11. In answer to your letter. I have given birth to a boy. He weighs ten pounds eleven ounces. Is this satisfactory?
12. You have changed my little boy into a little girl. Will this make any difference?
13. Please send my money at once as I have fallen into errors with my landlord.
14. I have no children as my husband is a bus driver and works day and night.
15. In accordance with your instructions, I have given birth to twins in the enclosed envelope.
16. I want my money quickly. I have been in bed with the doctor for a week and he does not seem to be doing me any good.

17. Milk is wanted for the baby and father is not able to supply it.
18. Re your kind enquiry. The teeth on the top are all right but the ones in my bottom are hurting terribly.

The following is another "funny" which causes much hilarity at parties. Usually the one who is trying to read it has to give up, overcome with mirth.

A Slight Misunderstanding

A young couple were searching for a house in the country. At last they decided on one which belonged to the vicar. On reaching home, neither of them could remember seeing the W.C. The young man wrote to the vicar, asking where the W.C. was, but the vicar, not being familiar with the abbreviation, thought they meant the Wesleyan Chapel, and replied accordingly:

Dear Sir,

I very much regret the delay in answering your letter. The nearest W.C. is seven miles away from the house, this is most unfortunate if you are in the habit of going regularly.

A number of people take their lunch with them and make a day of it. It is built to seat three hundred people and the committee have just decided to have plush seats installed for greater service and comfort. Those who can spare the time to walk, do so; others go by bus and train and get there just in time. The last time my wife went there was eleven years ago and she had to stand the whole of the time. It pains her not to go more often.

There are special arrangements for the children and ladies presided over by the vicar who will give every assistance possible within his power.

The children may sit together and can talk during the ceremony. I do hope this information will be useful to you both.

Yours faithfully.

P.S. Hymn sheets will be provided at the door.

CHAPTER SEVEN

Retirement. Quo Vadis? 1981-

I am now retired. I knew I should be lost if I did not make some effort to fill the unforgiving minute, so I hurled myself into every possible village activity. I have never been a "club woman" but I seem to be one now. I've joined the Women's Institute, the Red Cross and the Women's Voluntary Service to mention but a few.

Some of my neighbours have changed. When Joy and Peter left I said to them, "And what am I going to do without you? Who is going to come to my rescue whenever things go wrong?"

"Don't worry, Margaret," Joy laughed. "We've specially sold the house to a do-it-yourself man. You'll be all right."

After I had met Mary and John Callaghan, I rang Joy in her new home and thanked her for arranging such pleasant neighbours. They are so very helpful and kind.

My sister in Jersey was taken ill a few months before the last crisis began at the surgery. I have tried to visit her regularly and now of course I am more immediately available. As an O.A.P. I can travel half-price by boat and train and this is the way I go to Jersey these days. I find it tiring and a bit tedious, but by no means unbearable. The only worry is invariably, strike threats of railway or seamen. I think this is diabolic. Airports are so chaotic I am happier keeping my distance from them.

My cousin Rex died suddenly in 1979, and my other cousin, Basil, died even more suddenly a few weeks after I retired. One can be thankful that they were spared having to suffer long, lingering illness, but both these deaths came as a great shock to me. As one grows older one expects these things but I do not like to see the snapping links in the family chain.

I go swimming for exercise, cruising up and down with a dignified breast-stroke. I look with open envy at the young things who flash past me with their magnificent crawls.

I had hoped Mick would turn her hand to writing the best seller she had always promised us. She enjoys writing and has had a number of articles published in the past. So far she has been too busy setting her house in order and continuing to help all who are in trouble for miles around. I regret to says she looks as tired and worn as she ever did.

Mick is such a complex character. She is a real loner. When she was seventeen, she walked "The Road to the Isles" with only a volume of poetry for company. If she was not so totally unselfish, she would ask nothing more of life than to stay in her garden with her books and her music. The friendly, dedicated, compassionate doctor walks side by side with the shy academic. Another side of her is perhaps the most important of all. The devotion she has for her two sons. Not only has she been the most exemplary mother, but they are all real friends, which is comparatively rare today.

The elder will shortly be a qualified doctor. The younger, Jamie, whom I first met when he was about four, has grown up into a devastatingly attractive young man. He is in hotel management. I fell in love with this handsome little boy when he introduced himself to me at our first meeting. It is such a pity that I am more than forty years older than he is!

Mick and I are in complete agreement with so many other retired people who declare, "I can't think how I ever found time to go to work!"

As a final word, I would like to add, that like my other outstanding friend, Raymond Falla, in Guernsey, Dr. Mick Aylward, too, is a "legend in her own time". We shall never see their like again.

Badsey Evesham
July 1981-December 1981